How
To Start
Counseling

How

To Start

Counseling

WILLIAM EDWARD HULME is professor of pastoral theology and pastoral counseling at Wartburg Seminary, Dubuque, Iowa.

A native of Ohio, he received his B.S. from Capital University, his B.D. from the Evangelical Lutheran Seminary, and his Ph.D. from Boston University, where he served as a graduate assistant in the department of the psychology of religion. His training at Boston included work with the Institute of Pastoral Care at Massachusetts General Hospital, with the Charlestown State Prison, and with the Boston Dispensary.

At Wartburg College, where he served from 1949 to 1955 as college chaplain and head of the division of Christianity and philosophy, he was appointed to establish a voluntary pastoral counseling program for students. "For the first six weeks," Dr. Hulme says, "no student came. So I had to educate them in the various ways outlined in this book. Now they come with a momentum that keeps my office continually busy. I counsel with about 16 to 18 young people each week. And here I learned much of the procedure discussed in *HOW TO START COUNSELING.*"

Before coming to Wartburg, Dr. Hulme was for three years pastor of the Clinton Heights Lutheran Church in Columbus, Ohio. He is a frequent contributor to *Pulpit Digest*, the *Pulpit*, *Pastoral Psychology*, *Journal of Pastoral Care*, and other periodicals.

BUILDING THE COUNSELING PROGRAM OF THE CHURCH

William E. Hulme

ABINGDON PRESS
Nashville

HOW TO START COUNSELING

Library of Congress Catalog Card Number: 55-5735

Scripture quotations designated R.S.V. are from the Revised Standard Version of the Bible and are copyright
1946 and 1952 by the Division of Christian Education of the
National Council of the Churches of Christ in the U.S.A.

Chapters 1-3 and 6 are based on articles written by Dr.
Hulme in *Pastoral Psychology* and *The Pulpit*. Chapter 5
first appeared in the March, 1955, issue of *Pastoral Psychology*.

c

SET UP, PRINTED, AND BOUND BY THE
PARTHENON PRESS, AT NASHVILLE,
TENNESSEE, UNITED STATES OF AMERICA

Contents

CHAPTER ONE

The Problem

IT WAS MONDAY AFTERNOON. THE MEN WERE GATHERED IN THE social room of First Church. There was a speaker. His subject was pastoral counseling, and the pastors of the area conference were obviously interested. As he described the technique of counseling, however, he became increasingly aware of a mental cloud hanging over his audience. During the discussion period that followed, the trouble came out. Mr. Benson said it for the group: "Mr. Speaker, you have given us a lot to go on. And I for one am very appreciative. But my problem is to get them to come in the first place. I'm not exactly bowled over by people rushing to my door for counsel, as your talk would seem to indicate."

Mr. Benson sat down amidst a low chorus of amens. The problem was obviously common to many. Benson had a rural charge, with its rugged individualism of the American farmer. His brethren in the urban parishes, with their high-tensioned parishioners, felt the same way. At the close of the program the conference chairman told the speaker privately that if he knew the conference, he would also know why certain of the pastors were unable to get people to come to them. But the chairman could not dismiss the issue, for the problem was not confined to a few here and there. It was widespread.

The scene changes to a college chaplain's office. A student GI had dropped in to talk over his decision to change from the pre-theological course to social work. The chaplain asked him why he planned to make this change. "There's no use kidding ourselves," he said. "I want to do marriage and family counseling, and people just don't go to their minister with their problems. I honestly feel I can do more good for the church in this field outside the pastorate." He felt he knew the layman's side of it. The chaplain knew from his talks with students that there was more truth to what the young man said than pastors would like to admit.

But the pastor wants to counsel. He buys the current books on the subject, and he studies them. He makes a special effort to attend lectures and clinics on counseling. He has been stimulated in this interest by movements within the churches to get this counseling information to him. Clinical training centers are continuing to increase; seminaries are fostering institutes and academies on the subject. But comparatively little has been done with the problem of getting his people to come to him for this counsel that he is learning to give. Yet here is where the pastor meets his initial problem.

Some feel that not every pastor can be a counselor. One might also say that not every pastor can be a preacher. Yet he must preach. So also he must counsel. There are, of course, men who by past experience, temperament, and sensitivity are more adapted to counseling than others. Undoubtedly they make better counselors, even as men who are fluent, persuasive, and dynamic make better preachers. Whether he is naturally gifted as a preacher or not, the pastor profits from the study of homiletics; in like manner the gifted and not-so-gifted will benefit from the study of the principles of counseling. Just as surely as problems are not confined to certain pastors, so the counseling ministry cannot be limited to certain pastors. The people of the congregation, as well as others, need the pastor's counsel even though they do not come to him for it. They need help to take this first step.

Fortunately there is much that he can do to give them this help. There are definite steps that he can take to become a better counselor and to encourage his people to come to him. It is not the purpose of this book to teach the pastor to counsel. I shall, however, give him directions in securing this instruction if this is his need. The purpose of this book is to help the pastor reverse the trend among his people through a constructive approach that will bring them to him in their needs.

People Are Out of the Habit

When the pastor hears again and again of pastoral counseling and realizes that he himself is doing little counseling, he may begin to wonder if he is not an isolated case. He usually keeps his apprehensions to himself to avoid exposing himself as a failure before his brother pastors. Because he is sensitive to the responsibility of his position, he may blame himself for his dearth in counseling. He may be correct, at least in part. On the other hand, there is another factor that is involved. People as a whole are out of the habit of seeking their pastor's help in their problems. Even when they have serious problems, they may hesitate to talk about them because they are ashamed of them. They feel they are different for having such problems and cannot afford to let others know it—least of all their pastor. When I discussed the nature of my work as a pastoral counselor in a Christian college with a churchwoman, she said, "Why, I never would go to anybody with my problems—especially a minister. I would be too embarrassed."

To determine why people are out of the habit of going to their pastor with their problems would involve a project in research beyond the scope of this book. One can, however, point to some changes in our culture that undoubtedly are an influence in this direction. To say people are out of the habit implies they were once in the habit. Were people at one time accustomed to going to their pastor with their problems? There were great pastors in our past, men like Luther, Baxter, Oberlin, Drummond, Brooks, who were in constant demand as counselors. But there are also great pastors today. The question is whether the run-of-the-mill pastor of days gone by was also busy with counseling. From the nature of his role in society it would appear that he may have been. The pastor used to be the educated man in his community. His people came to him not only for spiritual counsel but often for legal and economic advice and even medical service. As a result the pastor was in the center of things, so far as the problems of his people were concerned.

With the educational advance in our times, the role of the pastor has moved from the center of community life to the periphery. No longer is a person encouraged by tradition to seek counsel from the pastor. Concomitant with this decline in pastoral influence was the increase in the competitive spirit in our culture, with its impetus to pride and its fear of weakness. This spirit has led to the isolation of the individual mind and to the concealment of sensitive feelings that should be shared. So long as people think there is a possibility that they can handle things themselves, they probably will not come to their pastor. Even when they are desperate, they may still stay away. The wife of one of my members asked for an appointment. After telling me how long she had debated whether or not she should come, she broke down and in near hysteria told me their marriage was breaking up. After I had counseled with her, I felt I should see the husband also. I went to *him*. After the problem had eased so that they thought they could work things out, I suggested that if he needed help again, he see me. He looked a little embarrassed and said, "I know I should have come to you before. I will try not to let my pride get in the way again."

The Need for the Pastor's Counsel

Ironically the characteristics of our age that drive people into the protective darkness of isolation also create the emotional disturbances that cause them to need counseling. We are living in an age when it is hazardous for people to withdraw into themselves. The tensions of wars and rumors of wars, the insecurity of our economy, the upheavals in the marital picture, the breakdown of the parent-child relationship, the frustrations inherent in getting to the top, the emptiness of spirit that comes from not belonging, and the religious impotence in the aftermath of scientism make it impossible for man to live alone. The breakdown of the close ties of a former age makes the pastoral relationship all the more necessary. Yet it is this very breakdown that raises the mental barriers that block an individual from entering into this relationship.

The anxious spirit of our age is concentrated in our larger cities, but it is found also in our rural areas and smaller towns. The metropolitan pastor knows only too well what commuter trains, apartment living, and office parties can do to an individual's approach to life. Norman Vincent Peale's complaint that people are so tense that he cannot put them to sleep with a sermon, is a distinctly urban situation. The rural pastor still finds it a challenge to keep the people who work in the fields all week awake in the pew on Sunday morning. Yet the age of tension has reached the rural areas. Doctors in rural and small-town communities have been finding a decided increase in psychosomatic disorders since the beginning of World War II. Bigger and better machinery has created greater opportunities for making big money and more anxiety over the greater gamble that is involved. That certain wholesomeness that comes from living close to the land is not enough to repel the destructive emotions that accompany any surrender to the competitive egocentricity of our culture. The rural or small-town pastor has the same need to do counseling as does the urban or suburban pastor. The former is handicapped even further, however, in getting his people to come to him for this counsel, because of the traditional independent spirit of the rural heritage.

The pastor's task, regardless of the location of his congregation, is to educate his people to come to him when they need help with their problems. There are too many broken homes that might have been saved if one of the members had gone to the pastor before the collapse. There are too many young people involved in immoralities who might have been spared had they confided to their pastor their starvation for affection. There are people in mental institutions who might not have been there if they had had a pastoral-counseling relationship when they needed it. There are too many church members who are going to their physicians for bodily ailments when they should be going to their pastors for the emotional ills behind these ailments. There are even more who are keeping their problems to themselves and whose psychic suffering grows worse because their harmful emotions have no therapeutic outlet. There is also the tragedy of wasted lives, undeveloped spirits, distorted values, and immature decisions that might have been prevented if these individuals had felt their way free to talk to their pastors when there was yet hope. There are limits to what counseling can accomplish, and it is part of the pastor's wisdom to recognize where other forms of therapy are needed. Yet anyone who has counseled or has been counseled according to the principles of pastoral counseling as it is currently understood knows what good can come from it and is gripped with the urgency of extending this benefit to others who need it badly.

The Scope of the Task

Before the pastor can educate his people to the counseling ministry, he must arrange for the mechanics of such a ministry. The physical setup for counseling plays an important role in its success. The schedule in time that is allotted to counseling is valuable not only as a needed structure for this ministry but also as an educative device in itself.

The goal of this educational process is to remove from our people's minds the barriers they have inherited from our culture that keep them from seeking the help of their pastor in their personal problems. It is a big job, and the pastor may not be able to do it alone, but he is the one who must take the initiative and set the machinery in motion. It is entirely within the realm of possibility and even probability that individuals who never seek our counsel in their problems can be persuaded to take this step. I have had people enter my office for counsel who I would have considered to be the last to come. They came because their resistance had been successfully counteracted by reason and persuasion.

The counseling ministry is not an isolated service of the pastor. What goes on in the total program of his ministry has much to do with his success or failure in getting his people to come to him. This relation of the counseling program to the other areas of the ministry begins in the pulpit. Here is where the majority of his people see and hear him most often. The sermon can either draw people to the pastor or create a barrier between him and them. It gives an idea of the way he would react.

The pulpit is a temptation to the pastor's ego. Before the rapt attention of his hearers he can set up his straw men and then proceed to knock them down with unchallenged finality. Although they may admire his eloquence or even his logic, the people with problems may wonder about his ability to understand. If there is a no-two-sides-to-the-story attitude in his preaching, they may feel they know what he would say anyhow. If he sounds as unbendable as a stone wall, they may fear his judgment upon them. If he preaches as though genuine Christians did not have problems—doubts, lusts, anxieties, resentments—his people will feel so guilty in having them that they would be afraid to bring them to his attention. On the other hand, if his sermons show an understanding of human problems and an attitude of love, these people will feel that he may understand *them* and also help them.

The pastor's calling ministry can also help to shape his people's opinion of him. It is something of a preview of the counseling process. Since his people are hesitant to come for counseling, they need this preview. The counseling ministry does not replace the calling program, since counseling grows out of calling. Just to call, however, is not enough; the preview may influence a person to stay away rather than to come. If the pastor is unable to keep a conversation moving, his parishioners may feel ill at ease in his presence. If he can talk freely but is not able to stimulate others to talk, his people may feel all the more incapable of expressing their problems to him. On the other hand, if the parishioner has enjoyed the visit and has participated in the conversation and found the pastor understanding and receptive, he is encouraged to make his problem the topic of conversation.

Nothing can wear a pastor down more than the organizational work of the ministry. Yet even in this administrative capacity his behavior has a direct bearing upon his counseling program. Working with people can be exasperating and frustrating. Since the minister is the most quoted person of the parish, what he says to Johnny Cuttup at the young people's society is told and retold from house to house with the usual amplifications. His patience and restraint at times when many a man would "blow his top" will benefit him in his counseling ministry. Often the people who irritate the pastor most are also those who have problems. His ability to transcend the conflict of the moment may mean the difference between opening and closing the door to future counseling with these people and also with others who would be offended by a peevish display on his part.

Every contact the pastor has with his people can be used to further his counseling program. Wherever he sees his people— on the street, in the store, at the game—he can aid his rapport by the warmth of his greeting. When we realize how much effort it takes for some of our people to come to us, we know

14

why these little things in conduct and contact can be so decisive. Students have come to my door and left without knocking. Some people take the telephone in hand to call for an appointment and then lose their nerve and hang up. The least discouragement in the process of their coming may be enough to veer them from their course. It may take a while to win their confidence sufficiently for them to bare to us the deep problems of their personal life.

It may not be too unfortunate that in this age of specialization ministers of counseling are not within the financial reach of most churches. While this office may seem to meet the needs where it has been tried, the unnatural division between preacher and pastor may block a natural avenue into the counseling room for some. The experience in the counseling room, on the other hand, is invaluable as a guide to the needs of the congregation. The preacher who counsels may find in his counseling ministry his greatest inspiration for his preaching. The pulpit is his means of extending his counseling ministry into the area of group therapy. Who knows how many problems we have prevented and heartaches we have healed through our sermons! The counseling ministry also has its beneficial effect upon the pastor's calling. Not only does it reveal to him the areas in need of his call, but it also tends to make him a more efficient caller. Any break between the pastor who calls and the pastor who counsels is a handicap, since calling may lead to counseling. The average pastor may do as high as eighty per cent of whatever counseling he does, during his calling. So the areas of the ministry have a reciprocal relationship to one another, and each is the loser when any one is neglected.

The Role of the Pastor's Personality

The personality of the pastor is an important factor in reaching his people. He is himself a part of the education. Methods are necessary, but they cannot stand alone. The principles of counseling, for example, are indispensable to the counselor, and yet they are empowered by the counselor's spirit. They cannot substitute for this spirit but are rather an effective expression of it. Beginning counselors usually go through a stage of learning where they become so conscious of technique that they become mechanical. Because they concentrate upon the proper wording of their response, they may cease to live for the counselee as interested personalities. Their counseling fails in spite of the method. So the educational procedure for getting people to come to their pastor with their problems cannot succeed apart from the character of the pastor.

Henry Drummond was one of the most natural counselors in the history of the ministry. He had a way of getting people to open their hearts to him in the shortest of time. People of all kinds, it is said, sensed intuitively that they could trust him. He had an empathy with troubled souls that was patterned after the compassion of Christ. As a result, he was continually in demand. Obviously Henry Drummond's personality accounts for his success as a counselor. Are the Henry Drummonds born that way, or can they be made?

Few of us can hope to be as naturally adapted to counseling as Drummond. Yet the philosophy of pastoral counseling is based on the premise that human nature can change—that personality handicaps can, to various degrees, be overcome and their wholesome counterparts developed. This is why the counselor counsels. His own philosophy applies also to him. He should not rule himself out as a candidate for counseling. It is imperative for him to understand his own problems before he can help others.

After asking whether I was acquainted with a certain counseling periodical, a pastor said, "Every time I read this magazine, I get depressed."

"Why?" I asked.

"The men who write these articles—they help people so much. They know just what to say and what not to say—and—well—it makes me realize what a blunderer I am. Frankly, it's frustrating!"

People who write in the field of counseling have their failures also. They, too, wonder if they are to blame when the counselee chooses to escape rather than face the issue, when he ceases to keep his appointments after a period of discouragement, when he slips back into old ways following what seemed to be an improvement. But people do not wish to hear about these failures, and so they do not write about them.

Much of what is said in this book was learned from the author's own errors. It is presented from the conviction that we not only can learn from our errors but can do much to overcome them. If it should open our eyes on occasion to some shortcoming in our approach, the purpose is not to depress but to show the way to improvement.

It is fundamental to the pastor's religion that power is available to give him sufficiency in all things so that he may abound unto every good work and present every man complete in Christ Jesus. Christianity is a religion of rebirth. There is an evangel for the captives: they can be set free through the grace of Christ from the destructive emotions that prevent their development into the fullness of his stature. They are not predestined to the inhibitions and failures of the past, for every part of their personality can be redeemed. The pastor as well as his counselee can become new.

The problem is in our inability to receive this power. The help from clinical psychology in removing the emotional blocks to the reception of grace is an example of how psychology and theology work together for the maturation of personality. The study of pastoral counseling is beneficial not only in equipping the pastor to counsel but also in his understanding of himself. The pastor can improve himself as a person and so become more attractive as a counselor. His spiritual, mental, and social experience can be guided into ways of growth.

We have reviewed the problem and surveyed the areas around which an approach can be developed to remedy the situation. We turn now to the task of developing this approach so that it may be applied by the pastor in an effort to bring his people to him for counseling. Our first area is the program of re-education.

CHAPTER TWO

Educating for Counseling

WHEN I WAS CALLED TO INITIATE A PASTORAL COUNSELING PRO-gram at a Christian college, I was confronted with the necessity of educating the student body to a counseling ministry. There simply was no other way that I could get the program going. I could sit in my office all day, but that alone would not bring anybody into the office. The students had to be shown what I was there for and why they might need my service.

So I began my educational program. It took six weeks before I noticed results. I utilized the printed page, personal contacts, classroom opportunities, and speaking appearances to inform the students concerning this ministry. Once the troubled in spirit began to come, the ministry was soon able to sustain itself through its own momentum. This did not mean that the educational emphasis was over, for each year well over a third of the student body consists of new students. Since the beginning days at college are difficult for these young people, I must begin immediately to educate them in the advisability of pastoral counseling.

The average pastor is not in the position where he is forced to call attention to his counseling ministry. In fact, there are many who would hesitate to attempt such a move because of modesty. To encourage people to avail themselves of their counseling ministry seems to them to be "tooting their own horns." It is as though the minister were trying to thrust himself into the lives of his people. This is because he considers the counseling ministry confined to himself as a person. He promotes other features of his church program. He invites people to attend Sunday-school classes, midweek Bible-study groups, and inquirers' classes where he is the teacher. He exhorts his people to attend church services regularly where he is the preacher. He is not bothered by modesty problems in these instances because there is more involved than himself. There are the Scriptures, the worship forms, and the music. Even though he plays a dominant role in these areas, he may still justify his promotion by his conviction that the Holy Spirit works through these means to bless his people.

It is precisely for this reason that he can tell his people about his counseling ministry. Jesus said to his disciples, "Receive the Holy Spirit. If you forgive the sins of any, they are forgiven; if you retain the sins of any, they are retained" (R.S.V.). The ministry is the human means through which the Holy Spirit works to heal the division within the soul. The office that was ordained to bring release from guilt and other destructive emotions was not to confine itself to group activity. The blessing of confession and forgiveness often requires the privacy of the personal ministry. The suffering that goes on within the minds of the people on our streets and in our pews is too often known only to God. These people need our help. It is for their sake that we educate concerning our pastoral counseling.

Some may ask, "Won't these problems often work themselves out without any counseling? Surely people must have had problems before we had all this emphasis on pastoral counseling. And they seemed to survive." Sometimes our problems seem to resolve themselves in the passage of time. More often, we may simply learn to live with them. They do not heal from the bottom but rather become permanent handicaps around which the personality shapes itself. There is no substitute for bringing one's problems to the light of day, where they can be viewed objectively. The counseling ministry is for those who have difficulty doing this by themselves. Our people need our encouragement to take advantage of this service in their needs. For love's sake it must be done. The counseling experience itself will convince both the counselor and the counselee of the value of this ministry and the necessity for extending its service.

Others may ask whether some of these problems are not beyond the pastor's ability to help. The answer may quite likely be yes. Yet the pastor may be able to direct these people to the source of help they need. And it is often because these people come to him in the first place that he both knows of their difficulty and has the influence to lead them to the needed therapy.

Guides to the Presentation of the Program

To establish his counseling program, the pastor must educate his people in the purpose of his ministry. This means that he invites them to talk over their problems with him and gives them reasons why they should do it. The aim is to present his counseling program in such a way that his people will see the wisdom in taking their problems to the pastor. His guide in doing this is a picture of the workings of the mind of an individual who is in need of counseling. Such a person often wants to talk to somebody but is hindered by fear from making the overture. One little remark may make the difference between whether he will come or not. He is afraid that he will not be able to express himself adequately and consequently will be misunderstood. He wonders how the pastor will react to his coming. He is afraid of what he will think of him after he tells him the embarrassing secrets of his soul. Sometimes also he is worried over whether the pastor will ever tell anybody else what he knows. Then again he wonders if it will really do any good to talk to him. In this state of sensitive ambivalence the pastor's presentation may tip the balance and bring him in.

The conception that many laymen have of pastoral counseling is one of the reasons they do not come. Whether it is justified or not, they still think of it in terms of a type of counseling that has bankrupted itself. They are not aware that a new emphasis has come out of the ruins of the traditional approach —one that is radically different from the view they hold. It is not the purpose of this book to present the methods of pastoral counseling. Yet it is necessary at this point to state briefly the principles behind the counseling process because of the role they play in the educational program. These principles are as follows:

1. The counselee is given an atmosphere of free expression so that he can air his problem as the counselor listens responsively.

2. As the counselee gives expression to the destructive emotions of guilt, fear, and resentment, he is relieved of their pressure, with the result that he can view his problem more rationally and gain insight into its nature and solution.

3. Throughout the entire process the counselor allows the counselee to retain the responsibility for his problem and its solution.

4. The counseling process is buttressed by the counseling relationship, which is in itself a stimulus for confidence.

5. The result is a growth of experience which not only makes possible greater insight but also enables the counselee to act on this insight for the solution to his problem.

The idea of counseling as advice is not popular with the people of today. And the pastor often gives the impression that advice is all that he can offer. "I know what he will say anyhow," they say, "so why go to him!" Even when the pastor is respected for his wisdom, there is the fear of obligating oneself in asking for counsel. Even though nothing is said by the pastor, these people feel under a pressure to follow the advice of one from whom they seek help. Rather than put themselves into this position, they may stay away.

This attitude reveals their ignorance of their own role in the counseling process. All the responsibility in the relationship seems to belong to the pastor. If their problem is one where little outwardly can be done to alter the difficulties, they may say, "Why should I go to him—what can he possibly do?" They fail to realize that counseling is a process wherein something happens to them so that they are able to handle their difficulties. It is the purpose of the educational program to replace their old and forbidding view of pastoral counseling with the new and attractive. This will gradually break down the idea that counseling is simply preaching. It also dissociates it from coercion.

A presentation that will meet these needs of the prospective counselee will vary in both its wording and its scope each time it is given, but it will include the following points in the total picture:

1. Express the sincere desire of the pastor to be of service. This gives to the anxious the reassurance that they need.

2. Show an understanding of how people feel who have problems. This strengthens their confidence that the pastor can help.

3. Explain the benefits of counseling in terms which people understand from their own experience. The goal is to help people to help themselves.

4. Testify to the resources of religion that enable the pastor to be more than a listener. The help he offers is more than a knowledge of psychology.

5. Assure them of acceptance and of the confidential nature of counseling. This is to overcome the barrier of embarrassment and shame.

6. Tell how to arrange for counseling. Ignorance in these practical details may be enough to prevent certain individuals from coming.

The following is a sample of such a presentation:

"As your pastor I would like to be of service to you in any way that I can. If you are having any difficulties that are causing you concern—if you feel the need to talk to somebody—you are more than welcome to come and see me.

"Most of us have problems at some time or other that seem a little more than we can handle by ourselves. It often helps if we can just talk to someone. If we keep our problems to ourselves, there is a danger that we may *keep* them. This is because our feelings get mixed up in our problems and our thinking becomes confused so that we cannot see the forest for the trees. When we talk our problems over with one whom we can trust, we bring them out from inside us. We get it off our chest and experience a feeling of relief. Then, because our problem has been laid on the table, as it were, we can see it more objectively and can more intelligently work out our solution.

"There is a tremendous power in our Christian faith to help us in our difficulties. We may, however, need guidance to know how to lay hold on this power and find our answers. You will be accepted as you are, and all that is told to me will be held in the strictest confidence. If you wonder if I will think your problem is important, remember this: if it is important to you, it *is* important, and it will be important to me. Call me or see me at any time for an appointment. My office hours are Tuesday and Thursday from 2 to 5 P.M. and Wednesday from 7 to 10 P.M., in the church office."

Occasions for Education

The invitation to counseling can be given most effectively after a sermon on personal problems. At such a time the pastor may introduce the subject by saying: "If any of you have some problem on your heart which you would like to talk over with your pastor privately, simply see me after the service or at any other time, and we will make an appointment. I would be very happy to serve you in this capacity, because I believe that it is in talking our problems over with one whom we can trust that we find our answers."

If it is not fitting to include the entire presentation of the counseling program at the church service, the invitation can be followed up by an explanation of the program in the parish paper or the Sunday bulletin. At less formal gatherings of his people the pastor may find opportunities to present the program in a more informative manner. For example, he is educating his people to start off with the proper conception of the ministry when he discusses his counseling in his inquirers' classes, membership or confirmation classes, or other instruction groups. Church organizational meetings, especially the young people's group, are also occasions for talking up the program. The place of youth in this educational emphasis is of such importance that it will be discussed in detail in a later chapter.

To impress upon his people the importance of his counseling ministry so that they will consider it as a normal resort in times of difficulties and will talk about it among themselves, the pastor should report on it even as he does his other functions. At quarterly, semiannual, or annual meetings of the congregation (or church council) he could give a report on the number of hours devoted to this personal ministry or the number of people with whom he has counseled. He should discuss it with his official congregational leaders, in an attempt to reach each individual in the area of the congregation who needs help. He could ask them for suggestions on how he could bring this ministry to the attention of his people. In this manner he encourages them to feel it is a congregational task in which each interested member should assume his responsibilities.

He can, however, talk about it too much. All promotion can be overdone. It is like evangelism. We can bear our witness to the same individual too often and lose our effect. So when the same people hear about the counseling ministry too much, the appeal is weakened. If the pastor carries it even further, it may become a standing joke. "Here we go again!" they may say. This "overpromotion" gives people the impression that the pastor is trying too hard—that he needs to get people to come to him to satisfy his own desire for success—or that the program is not working out so well.

Consequently, it is best to vary the direct invitations with casual references here and there to the counseling ministry. He could, for example, recommend a self-help book, or even give a review of it at an organizational meeting, and comment that through his own experience in counseling he has found this or that suggestion in the book to be sound. This type of indirect approach may have a positive effect upon those who have a resistance to doing what someone else suggests. These would especially include those individuals who have a large amount of resentment.

The pastor may find it helpful on occasion to use lay leaders in his educational program. I was pushed into this procedure and found it quite effective. Having to be absent from the campus during freshman orientation, I secured the services of an upperclassman who was one of my former counselees to present the counseling program to the new students. A change in persons seems to diminish the danger in repetition without losing the advantages. Repetition is an aid to education and persuasion. Coming from somebody else on occasion makes the message somewhat new for those who have heard it before.

The Satisfied Counselee

The educational program accomplishes two objectives simultaneously. Presenting the structure of the counseling relationship not only gives an *invitive* picture of counseling but also conditions the counselee for his own role. It is always a big hurdle for the counselor to get his counselee to take the responsibility for his problem. If he comes already realizing that the counseling process is to help him to get his own understanding into his problem and find his own solution, the counseling will normally take less time than otherwise and will be far more pleasant for both the pastor and the counselee. Even though people like the idea of being free to make their own decisions, they may be tempted to shy away from this responsibility when the time comes. If they have been informed beforehand in the pastor's philosophy in this respect, they are less likely to try to maneuver him into taking their responsibility when the old regressive patterns exert their pressure.

Counselees who have been helped will tell others about the pastor's counseling ministry. The report will get around: "You ought to talk with the minister sometime. You don't necessarily have to have a problem. It just does something for you to talk with him." If the pastor counsels according to the principles of pastoral counseling, his counselee will at least be confronted with an atmosphere conducive to growth. The degree to which he is helped will depend upon whether his problem is within the scope of pastoral counseling and upon his own readiness for help.

There is a difference between helped and solved. Those whose problems are old and deeply buried do not overcome them by a few sessions with the pastor; they may, however, receive some release and some insight. The counselee who has not yet suffered enough or who lacks the determination to overcome his problem can scarcely make rapid progress, but he may gain the satisfaction from the counseling relationship that will bring him back at a later date. Mrs. Henderson, for example, came to talk about a religious problem. She had trouble with doubts and asked such intellectual questions as, "What is faith?" The pastor was aware that there was more to her problem than she was either able or desirous to bare. She was ready to discontinue the counseling after she noticed some degree of improvement. A few months later she returned for counsel in a serious marital problem. Her previous counseling experience had conditioned her for this return.

Not all those who receive counseling may appreciate its value. A few may even resent both it and the counselor because the process confronts them with realities they prefer not to recognize. This is particularly true when the counselor goes beyond the principles of counseling by probing and suggesting. Even this resentment is often only temporary. The majority will experience a satisfaction that leaves them favorably disposed toward counseling with the pastor. As they mingle with people at a level we pastors can scarcely approach, they will discover those who need help. "Why don't you talk to the pastor?" they will say. "I did myself a while back, and I know it helps."

Pitfall for the Pastor

The fact that his satisfied counselees are his best public relations is an occupational hazard to the pastor who is attempting to establish a counseling ministry. The necessity of making a good impression with the counselee puts him under a strain. Growing anxious lest he fail to "satisfy his customer," he may assume the responsibility both for the interview and for the problem. His concern over his own role divides his attention so that he is unable to concentrate as a listener. The result is that he undermines the impression he wants to make by departing from the principles of counseling. The counselee does not gain the satisfaction from the counseling process that it was meant to give. Realizing this, the counselor becomes less confident than before.

The answer to this danger is the faith that comes out of experience—experience with God and experience with counseling. The pastor has a method that is sound—one that will prove itself repeatedly as he grows in understanding it and becomes proficient in using it. The pastor has a God who works through the method to effect its results—a God who is bigger than the method and can succeed in spite of the pastor's blunders. It is his faith in both of these that keeps his own inner dynamics in order. In this way he can safeguard his motives from becoming self-centered when he becomes acutely aware of his inadequacy.

The security of such a faith opposes the anxiety to please in the counseling process.

This faith is nurtured in the pastor's prayers for his people and in particular for his counselees and those who he feels should be his counselees. Prayer is both a result of and a stimulus to trust in God. The counselee is particularly blessed whose pastor intercedes for him before the throne of grace in his own private chamber. The scourge of anxiety, however, can enter even into our prayer life, so that the pastor's motivation in his intercession may become confused between his emphatic concern for his people and his concern for his own success as their pastor. Of course, he needs God's help for both. Because the concern over his own role is likely to be charged with fear, however, it tends to endanger his disinterested concern for his people. It may disturb him that in his own mind his counselees seem to serve as the means to his success rather than as the end to which his success serves as a means. We can rejoice that God nowhere in His Word sets up purity of motive as the qualification for receiving his blessing in the ministry. If this were true, none of us could expect to be used of him. All of us owe whatever success we have to the grace of God. Something so subtle as purity in motive cannot be guaranteed by any technique. Yet there is a procedure in prayer which at least does not encourage the corruption of the self-center and which we shall discuss in the chapter on developing the spiritual life.

Educating the people concerning the counseling ministry extends also to the mechanics of the program. The time and place of counseling, as well as other physical details, contribute toward this end. We turn next to the physical arrangements for counseling.

CHAPTER THREE

The Mechanics of the Program

EDUCATION CONCERNING THE COUNSELING MINISTRY MAKES it clear to the people that the pastor is available to help them. Our people think that we pastors are very busy. And we are. Because they realize this, they may be reluctant to take us away from our work to talk about their problems. People with problems are often fearful people, and if they are not sure that we can spare the time or that we want to spare it, they may stay away. When the pastor publicly invites them to come, it is obvious that he has the time and that they are welcome.

Regular Hours

Even though one wishes to be available at all times, it is usually advisable to have regularly designated hours for counseling. Not that the pastor will confine his counseling to these hours or to his study, but he will concentrate upon his counseling ministry at these times. The posting of such hours in the church bulletin helps to keep the counseling ministry before the people; it is a constant reminder of their opportunity. They realize that the pastor expects them to come to him and that he considers it important enough to set aside a certain amount of his time for it. This assures those who have problems that they are not such isolated cases after all. "Maybe there are others like me," they say to themselves. "Then perhaps he won't think I'm such a mess if I tell him my trouble. If he is devoting several hours a week to counseling, others must actually be going to him." These hours also give them the assurance that if they call during this time, they will not be interrupting him from anything more important, nor will they experience any of the other embarrassments that come with calling at the wrong time.

This posting of counseling hours carries the implication that the people themselves must take the initiative in getting help. The pastor is announcing when he is available; the next move is up to them. While the pastor must never cease going to his people, he must also never cease encouraging them to come to him. If they will take this step, they are making an effort to be helped. Since they are assuming the responsibility for initiating the counseling, they are more likely also to take the responsibility for their problem. The possibilities for helping an individual are probably fifty per cent greater when he voluntarily comes for counseling than when the pastor must go to him. Nevertheless, there are times when the pastor has to make the contact. This problem will be taken up in a later chapter. Whatever encourages people to come on their own will contribute to the positive result of the counseling.

While it may seem that the burden is placed on the counselee to arrange his time to fit into the hours the pastor has selected, this is actually an advantage for the counselee. If a person has to give of himself, he is more likely to get something in return. If he were going to a medical or psychiatric doctor, he would have to pay. The fact that he would make a financial investment tends to increase both his appreciation and his co-operation. The pastor, of course, has no fee. His counselees, however, must invest their time. He need not feel guilty if in cases of conflicting time schedules his counselee has to give a little here and there to arrange an appointment. This additional effort on the counselee's part is an indication of his determination.

Having regular hours for counseling is a help to the pastor, too. He himself is in a dilemma when his people come at the wrong time. If someone he has been hoping would come arrives fifteen minutes before he must leave for an important meeting, he is immediately in conflict. He may hesitate to tell this person that he can only talk to him for a few moments, and at the same time feels constrained to keep his engagement. The result often is that he procrastinates in making the decision in the hope that fifteen minutes will take care of it. The tension continues to mount within him as he tries to hurry things along. Whenever one tries to hurry the counseling process, he misses his cues, gets ahead of his counselee, and ends up slowing the process. Apprehensively he may steal a glance at his watch. The counselee notices it and says, "Perhaps I'm taking too much of your time." It all happens too quickly for the pastor to say anything but, "Oh, no, no—just go right ahead." And the situation continues even more tensely than before.

If he has a certain time set aside for counseling, his mind is relieved of the pressure that he should be doing something else. Giving a time structure to one's activities counteracts tension. It gives him the feeling that things are under control— that all is planned and accounted for. It is advisable to allot approximately an hour to an appointment. Not that an hour will always be needed, but if it is, the time is available. And if the problem has any depth, an hour will be needed. It takes about half an hour simply to get through the surface layers to some of the basic issues.

The times when the pastor will schedule his counseling hours will depend upon the individual congregation. There is little value in having hours when the majority of his people are at work. The industrial areas with their shifts, the rural areas with their chore times, the suburban areas with their commuters, call for special consideration. Some of the hours should be in the evening so that those who cannot come during the day will still have the opportunity. To schedule another activity for the evening may seem impossible for the busy pastor's schedule. The ministry is becoming more and more concentrated in evening activities. The pastor may have to sacrifice a meeting or two to have counseling hours at least once a week in the evening. A choice that enables him to do more personal work ought at least to be the lesser of two evils. The pastor who is in the process of establishing a counseling program may not always be busy during these hours. Nevertheless, he should remain in his office or other designated place during this time; otherwise people may call when he is not there and become confused over his availability for counseling.

Suitable Place

I know of a pastor who is trying to establish a counseling program and whose only place to counsel is a combination ante-room and storage place at his church. There is a door at each end of the room. Boxes and file cabinets line the walls, and his large desk almost fills the available space. He never knows (nor does the counselee) when some well-meaning parishioner may descend upon him in search of something, or in going from one room to another. To do a good job at counseling, you need a suitable place.

This means first of all a place that will insure privacy. A room will do this, whereas a hallway will not. The idea of being enclosed by four walls gives a feeling of safety to one who has something to say concerning which he is very sensitive. Even the approach to the counseling room should be as private as possible. The slightest doubt over whether whether they will be protected from the eyes and ears of others will keep many potential counselees away. Often they have an exaggerated sense of shame over their problem, and what little security they have depends on keeping their disgrace concealed. This is why it is so difficult for them even to go to a counselor. Whatever threatens to expose their vulnerable area to others creates a feeling of terror. Even for others to know they are going to a counselor causes them to feel exposed. My office at college is

33

in the balcony of an auditorium, and classes often met in the auditorium during my counseling hours. Many a student backed out at the foot of the stairway to the balcony rather than risk being on display as he entered the chaplain's office. I had to have a screen erected to eliminate this ordeal for the sensitive who have problems.

An office at the parsonage is handicapped by this danger to privacy. The presence of the pastor's family and the eyes of his neighbors are an obstacle in the mind of the self-conscious counselee. When the parsonage is constructed so that the pastor's study is shut off from the rest of the house and has its own entrance from the outside, the difficulty is lessened. The church, however, has advantages for counseling that are not possible for the parsonage. It is a semipublic building, and even outsiders feel they have a right to enter. To the member the church is the center of religious life and the scene of sentimental and sacred memories—the house of the Lord, where the Holy Communion is celebrated. The chancel of worship and symbol, so conducive to religious feelings, is available when needed. Some find it helpful to enter the sanctuary with the counselee for prayer when assurance of God's forgiveness, comfort, or help is greatly needed.

A hole in the wall, however, even if it is in church, is not the answer. Because people are susceptible to suggestion, they are uplifted by the attractive and depressed by the barren. Our surroundings affect our spirits in a subconscious way. The counseling room should be large enough so that two individuals will not feel cramped in it. When space is limited, one can use ingenuity in the furnishings. Everything that is excess baggage should be removed. A small desk and two ordinary-size chairs are all that is necessary. The furniture should be attractive even though simple, the room well lighted and having light-colored walls, and the temperature comfortable. Except for those who appreciate antiques, old furniture has a forbidding appearance;

on the other hand, furnishings that have a new appearance tend to be uplifting. Pictures on the wall proportionate to the size of the room can improve the appearance; pictures of Christ contribute to the atmosphere of pastoral counseling. The room should be arranged so that when the door is opened, the counselee is not exposed to the view of whoever has knocked. An outside entrance to the study offers an easier and more private approach.

Finding a suitable place for counseling will for most pastors be a matter of making the most of what one has and looking for something better. So far as the former is concerned, women are often better at this than men. If the pastor has his wife study his counseling room, and follows her suggestions for its improvement, he probably will end up with a reasonably attractive place. In regard to the latter—the search for something better—it is well to remember that what the congregation invests in, it takes an interest in. If more churches were encouraged to provide the pastor with a counseling room, they would be more conscious of its importance and more likely to take advantage of it. In view of all that may be gained, the pastor can put aside his reluctance to ask his congregation for financial as well as creative help for his counseling ministry.

Succeeding with the Program

When Miss Betty Brown asks for an appointment, she may have a "few butterflies in her stomach." She will look for signs that show her she is welcome. It is encouraging to be received in a gracious manner. The pastor's facial expression can do a great deal to reassure her. If she calls on the telephone, she will be sensitive to the sound and inflection of his voice. Nothing can give a cooler impression than a businesslike "yes" or "no" on the phone. It is the little things to us that are big things for the hypersensitive. If we can put ourselves in their place and try to make it as easy as we can for them, they will be much more able to talk. Anything that radiates a warm personality gives the green light to go ahead.

I have had the experience more than once of hearing footsteps approaching my office, and instead of hearing the expectant knock on the door, I have heard the footsteps departing. Later I learn what happened. Someone will say, "I was over to see you, but before I could knock, I lost my nerve and left." When Miss Brown arrives, she will probably be tense and hesitant. The pastor can help her by giving her a smile, asking for her coat, and directing her to a chair. The best way to put someone else at ease is to be at ease yourself. A little small talk about the latest news or even the weather may help. To prolong this kind of chatter, however, may create a problem in itself—namely, how to get down to business.

Since Miss Brown may feel somewhat helpless in the situation, the pastor can guide things by saying, "Well, Miss Brown, I take it you have something you wish to talk over with me."

This may not be sufficient if the counselee is blocked by anxiety over introducing her problem. If she says, "There are really three things I came to see you about," the pastor can reasonably assume that it is the third one that is important and that he can dispense with the first two in short order. Yet he needs to be patient with the seemingly unimportant conversation of his counselee, for it will probably lead him sooner or later to what is important. If he tries to force the issue by prodding the counselee, he may only increase the blockage. And if he decides to bring the interview to a close because it is unimportant, he may force the counselee to talk, but on the other hand he may also force her to leave. If she had something more important to talk about, it would be very difficult for her to return.

Prolonged small talk may also result when the pastor is subconsciously reluctant to face the discouraging facts. His need to hear the good about his people may be counteracted by the counselee's need to emphasize the negative. His desire to see improvement in his counselee is at times matched by the counselee's resistance to admit any improvement. When the pastor senses such a situation, he may use small talk as an indirect attempt to cheer up the counselee so that the actual counseling will be more pleasant. This only postpones the ordeal. He is fortunate if his counselee brings him down to earth by saying, "But this isn't what I came here for."

Naturally he wants to help Miss Brown. He may even fear that he will fail her. Let him pause to remember that he is not alone in his counseling. There is always the great Counselor, whose presence and power are more than a complement to the inadequacies of the pastor's human nature. This does not mean that he can substitute his trust for his own lack in skill. It does mean that even with our skill, our reliance is upon God. If the pastor makes the effort to equip himself for counseling and counsels as well as he can according to the principles of the science and the resources of his religious heritage, he can ask the Lord to guide him and trust his work will be blessed. Because he has been a good listener as well as a sympathetic friend, his counselees may say to him, "I've come here feeling pretty low, but I always seem to leave feeling better."

As the pastor counsels with Miss Brown, the intimate details of her life will become part of his thinking. She needs assurance that what she has revealed to him will be held in the strictest of confidence. His verbal assurance is meaningless unless it is backed up by the facts. The rule that the pastor reveals nothing that is said to him in confidence is all too often violated. He does not deliberately talk about these things; they slip out in a moment of carelessness at the family table or in the company of friends. When our wives or children or brethren inadvertently let things slip in ever-widening circles, the damage is done. Although our marriage is the closest of human relationships, even to tell our wives things given to us in confidence is a betrayal of this confidence. Though in our own eyes our wife is one with us, in the eyes of others we are two different people. It is also unfair to place our wives in the position of knowing too much. Even though they say nothing, the fact that they know interferes with the naturalness of their relationship with these people.

No pastor wants to betray a confidence. Yet we are under pressures that at times undermine our good intentions before we realize it. It may help to understand the nature of these pressures so that we may be alert for the danger.

To be "in the know" concerning the lives of others is flattering to the ego. When the pastor hears others talking about somebody or something concerning which he has inside information through his counseling, he is tempted to impress his hearers with what he knows. This urge is particularly strong when these others are acting as though they knew all about the subject but obviously do not. If he succumbs to the temptation to set them straight and then realizes what he has done, he may attempt through more talking to redeem the situation or at least to justify it. The usual result is that he gets himself in deeper. After one has done a certain amount of listening to the sound of his own voice, he reaches a state of conversational intoxication. Information that would never have passed through his lips at the beginning of the conversation now slips out with surprising ease.

The pastor needs an outlet even as do others. Yet in "letting down his hair" with the members of his family, intimate parishioners, or ministerial friends, he should draw the line on information given to him in confidence. He also must be careful about discussing information which, though not techincally of a confidential nature, is still not for public ears. Once the pastor gets the reputation of not being able to keep a confidence, his counseling program is ended. He had better make plans to move to another church and start over again to remedy his error. Even as a talebearing tongue is a liability to the pastor in his counseling, his reputation as one who is *closelipped* about the private affairs of others is an asset to the program.

After Miss Brown has talked over her problem and the pastor has listened responsively, she may feel exceptionally good. After one has got something "off his chest" that has been bothering him for some time, the relief is exhilarating. Miss Brown may feel everything has cleared up. The pastor is wise to suggest a follow-up appointment. Getting rid of the negative feelings is not necessarily the same as solving the problem; it may be only the first step if the issues that caused the negative feelings in the first place are still alive. When Miss Brown returns, the pastor may discover there is still need for counseling. Now that the initial good feeling has leveled out, the counselee realizes that the conflicts that gave rise to her emotional disturbance are still present.

I am convinced that the most common failure of pastors who have some knowledge of the principles of counseling is their neglect to follow up the initial interview. If the problem has any depth to it, it cannot be solved in one session. The pastor may leave the door open for the counselee to return but in such an indefinite way that nothing comes of it. Or if the counselee does return, it may be after such a long interval that the second interview is unable to build upon the earlier session.

Regardless of how much may seem to have been accomplished in the initial release of pressure, the pastor should arrange a follow-up in words something like the following: "Would you like to come back and see me next week—just to see how things are going? We can make it this same hour."

He will usually find his counselee quite willing. He may say, "Are you sure I'm not taking too much of your time?" which is another way of saying, "I'd like to come if I'm sure you want me to." The number of interviews depends upon the nature of the problem. Once the results of catharsis have been assimilated —usually after the first and second interviews—the danger of ceasing the relationship too soon is lessened. It is like entering the adjustment stage of a courtship following the period of infatuation. The increasingly realistic understanding of the situation prevents any illusion. The pastor should structure his counseling relationship with follow-up interviews in sufficient quantity to enable the counselee to cope with the exigencies of life on his own.

CHAPTER FOUR

Beginning with Youth

IF WE WERE TO INTERVIEW THE PASTORS OF AMERICA AND ASK them in what area they find their greatest need for counseling, they would undoubtedly answer—marital problems. This was also my experience, but when I left the parish ministry for the college chaplaincy, the picture changed. Marital problems were in the minority, and the familiar problems of youth were predominant. For a while I wondered whether I was out of the main stream of pastoral counseling, but I soon realized I was really in the headwaters. What actually are marital problems? They are problems that have their origin within the personality structure of one or both of the marital partners, and they merge as marital problems in the challenging adjustment of married life. Because of their new appearance they cause us to lose sight of their previous history. If people who are having these marital crises could have had the benefits of pastoral counseling before they became married, they might have prevented much of their present difficulty.

The pastor who counsels with his youth and helps them to overcome the deformities in their souls is contributing to happy marriages in the future. Not only will these young people who have been helped to solve the problems of their personalities make better marital partners, but they will also make better parents. Since parents are the most important influence in the development of their children, whatever contributes to better parents contributes to the emotional security of their children.

Counseling with youth is the ounce of prevention that is worth the pound of cure. The more the pastor is able to get his young people to come to him with their problems, the less his counseling will be needed in the ventures of their future.

There is so much emphasis on problems today that little attention is given to the pastor's preventive ministry. Unlike the physician, who deals primarily with the ill, the pastor works also with the healthy. He is able to minister to them in ways that prevent their becoming ill. The pastor receives little, if any, recognition for this service, since its scope is known only to God. In moments of discouragement he may become more objective in his view by recalling to mind this large but noncredit area of his ministry—not as an escape, but as a balance.

The pastor who counsels with his people while they are still in their youth is using his influence to its greatest possible effect. He is getting to them while they are still in their developing years—at a time when they are in the process of making the great decisions of life: the choice of a goal in life, of a particular vocation, and of a marital partner. Whatever influences the development of their personality will be a decisive factor in making these choices which have so much to do with the quality of their future life. The place of youth in pastoral counseling has the same significance as the place of youth in evangelism: only two per cent of the people are won for the church after the age of twenty-five. The structure of the personality hardens with age, so that only the violence of shock may alter its pattern.

Youth is also a time of great suffering. The painful awareness of their own inadequacies, together with their extreme sensitivity to the opinions of others concerning them, stimulates the destructive emotions of guilt, anxiety, and resentment within young people to violent intensities. Although we may speak of the traumas of youth with a smile, they are anything but humorous to those who are experiencing them. Rejection by classmates, failure to have dates, the broken romance, friction with parents, guilt over sex, incompetence in sports, torture the minds of young people. Their suffering is particularly critical because their personalities are in the molding process, and if these wounds do not heal properly, the emotional disturbance may continue as a pattern of reaction that will hinder their growth. Youth need pastoral counseling for the relief from suffering and for the prevention of emotional problems in adulthood.

Getting Them to Come

The pastor who wants to establish a counseling ministry needs to direct his educational program with special emphasis toward his young people. Some pastors schedule personal interviews with their young people to prepare the way for counseling. These appointments can be made by mail or by personal contact. It usually helps to create a receptive attitude toward these interviews if the pastor announces his plan in a general way beforehand. This can be done during the assembly at Sunday school, at the young people's society, or in confirmation or premembership instruction classes. Those who use this method often make it a practice to have such an interview with each young person in the congregation at least once a year. The time suggested should be one convenient for the young person, such as immediately following school. My own card of invitation is:

Dear John:
This is an invitation to come to my office at the church at 3:30 P.M. on Wednesday, so that we may have a visit together.
If this is not convenient for you, would you contact me prior to the time to arrange for another appointment.

Sincerely yours,
Your Pastor
(signature)

There is a potential value for counseling in anything that brings pastor and parishioner together. The interview plan, however, requires skillful handling or it can boomerang. Because it is prearranged rather than spontaneous, the interview may begin on an artificial note. The danger is that it may become fixed on this note. The key figure in the interview is the pastor. Because he arranged the visit, he feels responsible for its success. The initial stiffness may cause him concern, so that he begins to do too much of the talking. If the young person is one who finds it difficult to express himself, the session may easily degenerate into a "man-on-the-street" type of interview: the pastor asks the questions, the young person gives an answer, the pastor adds his commentary, and then the process begins all over again. The interview ends when the pastor runs out of questions. Although all of this may be accompanied by an affable spirit, it gives the wrong impression of what counseling with the pastor would be like. Because of the tension the pastor has directed the interview, and the young person has been denied an introduction to the principles of counseling.

Although the pastor may have to start the interview on its way, it is only as one would prime a pump. His objective is to encourage the interview to carry along on its own momentum. When he is able to pattern his conversation according to the principles of counseling, he will be succeeding in his goal. If the young person has a problem that is disturbing him, this kind of interview may often end up in a counseling situation. The pastor may subconsciously prevent this from happening. He is psychologically ready for a social interview and not a counseling session. He may resist the momentum of the interview from entering a counseling stage by passing up any clues the young person may give that everything is not quite right in his life. Determined to keep to his role as an amiable interviewer, the pastor structures the interview to keep it free from any "depressing business."

He can prevent the transition to counseling also by looking for a problem. The young person may be already suspicious that the interview is an indirect attempt on the part of the pastor to counsel him. If the pastor gives the impression that he is probing for a problem, he will only confirm this suspicion, and the young person may become defensive and clam up. This will not happen if the pastor allows the interview to be its own guide and is alert for any subconscious attempt on his part to control it.

Another plan for getting on closer terms with young people is to invite groups of them over to the parsonage for informal discussion and refreshments. This lacks the personal element of the interview method, but it is less artificial. It gives the young people a chance to talk with the pastor in a conversational way and may encourage them to continue the conversation in private. The informality of the occasion strengthens the rapport of their relationship so that they are less hesitant to ask him for an appointment.

Unlike the interview method, invitations for the group session had better be given in person. Since the young people know that others beside themselves are involved, there is less pressure to be present. Also, the fact that the session may likely be held in the evening makes the chances for a conflict in engagements greater. To avoid absences in these group meetings, the pastor may find it advisable to allow the young people alternatives in the choice of a time so that all may attend. There is also a greater obligation to attend when one has had a voice in the selection of the time.

Using the Young People's Organization

The usual organizational structure for the young people of the congregation offers excellent opportunities for the pastor to reach his youth with his counseling ministry. I refer particularly to the young people's Sunday-school class and the young people's society. The topics for study or for the program can easily be directed into those areas that relate to the problems of young people. These problems have a consistency that makes it easy to construct a program around them. Of course, any attempt to classify youth problems would be an oversimplification, since problems with any depth center in the emotions and have their repercussions in many areas of a person's life. A young person whose problem has its origin in a conflict with his parents may experience difficulty in his social adjustments because of it. This in turn may lead him into sexual problems over which he develops guilt feelings, and he may finally come to his pastor disturbed over his religious doubts. Nevertheless, whatever is a help to this young person in any one area of his problem will have a beneficial influence in all the areas. These major areas in which young people experience their problems are as follows:

Emotional instability. Although any serious problem is disturbing to the emotions, people who are emotionally unstable are chronic sufferers. The cause of their emotional chaos is overshadowed by the chaos itself. They are so lacking in security that their inner life is in constant agitation.

Social difficulties. Youth are particularly sensitive about their place in their own group. Because their acceptance by others means so much to them, they tend to magnify their social inferiorities and failures. They are extremely curious over how others evaluate them and are easily depressed if others seem to slight them.

Problems over sex, courtship, and marriage. Confusion over what is normal and abnormal, or right and wrong, concerning the rise of sexual attraction during the period of youth may cause young people tremendous anxiety and guilt.

Family difficulties. Since family relationships are the strongest influence in the development of personality, whatever is lacking in these relationships undermines the security, confidence, and incentive of young people.

Problems in religion. Young people are acutely aware that they need a religious faith. However, their expanding intellectual powers appear as a threat to this faith. Any emotional conflict at this time aggravates this problem because it is a block to the emotional phase of religious experience.

Adjustment to the Atomic Age. The ominous future of military service and atomic, hydrogen, and cobalt bombs hangs over our youth and provokes whatever insecurity there is within them into serious problems of morale. The entire problem of vocation is influenced by this tension of our times.

Problem of vocation. The selection of a particular vocation rests upon the confidence the youth has in himself and in his understanding of his own purpose in living. Vocational information, testing programs, and even the Christian concept of calling, must cope with the emotional situation created by the other areas.

Usually the pastor has ample opportunity to address his young people's groups. If he selects a topic in one of these trouble zones, he will not only be giving his youth help where they need it most, but will be stimulating them to come to grips with their problems and to consider seeking his pastoral counsel. At the same time he may find himself boosting both the interest and the attendance in these groups. Young people are "personality conscious"; words like "inferiority complex" and "self-confidence" have a high emotional appeal. Topics centering around the Christian approach to a radiant and triumphant personality "catch fire" with youth.

Contrary to current opinions, our young people do not know too much about sex. Often they are tragically ignorant of the Christian interpretation of sex. In spite of our greater emphasis on sex education, many of our Christian youth have mixed feelings over sex. Our culture has encouraged an affinity of sex for guilt.

The feeling that sex is at best only tolerated by God may be too strong to be driven out by intellectual education. The innocent victims of sexual perverts often feel a sense of shame in simply having been involved in the affair. They may even hesitate to tell anybody of the experience. Even though we are living in a day when sex is discussed openly in a spirit of adolescent abandon, sex and secrecy still go together in the society of the church. Such secrecy only adds to the association of sex with guilt. Sex is a power, and when it becomes associated with guilt in a person's mind, it tends to become an uncontrollable power. Because of this, he may grow to fear it. The destructive emotions of guilt and fear act as magnets upon our attention. The result may be a fixation upon sex that leds to morbid imaginings for which the young person can only condemn himself. It is this condition of mind that is the impetus for masturbation as well as fornication. It also has its influence in the widespread indulgence in heavy petting among young people whose respect for the commandment preserves their virginity in at least its literal meaning.

A talk or series of talks or studies on the Christian interpretation of sex by the pastor is greatly appreciated by young people. Anyone who shows an understanding of this subject has a unique appeal to them that spontaneously draws them to him and his counseling.

The same is true of its related topic of courtship and marriage. Young people face disturbing questions in this area and will not only be enlightened by the pastor's guidance but will also be encouraged to consult with him in their courtship problems. When they become ready for marriage, they are also more likely to plan for the pastor's premarital counseling, which is an improvement over the usual procedure where the pastor must suggest premarital counseling after the couple inform him they desire to be married—often the next week. When there is premarital counseling, particularly on a voluntary basis, the pattern is begun for seeking later help if this becomes necessary. Many a rift between husband and wife has been healed because they knew where to go when their difficulties arose, and were mentally receptive to going.

Although the pastor may not feel he can speak directly on parental and family problems when he is also the pastor of the parents, he can nevertheless indicate in his discussion of other youth problems that he understands parental conflicts and that he recognizes parental frailties. The study of Christian doctrine, if it is applied to their own religious needs, has an appeal for young people that invites counseling. I have found that my classes in Christianity are one of my best feeders for my counseling program. The stability of the Christian religion is attractive to youth who are insecure, and is a challenge to their need for a faith to inspire them. The ever-pressing problem of choosing a vocation often rests upon this inner instability that is religious in nature. They seek a purpose they can trust, something they can identify themselves with and strive toward.

The social hour following a young people's meeting—or for that matter, any gathering—offers the pastor an excellent opportunity to engage in personal conversations that may lead to counseling. During or following refreshments the group's attention is broken down into units of individuals, couplets, trios, and quartets, so that the pastor may easily move among the group to engage in successive private conversations with individuals. Since others are absorbed in conversation, he can do this without being conspicuous. Since minds have already been stimulated by the topic and the mood is one of fraternization, he will have little trouble initiating such conversations. In fact, he may find himself being drawn to the side by the individuals themselves.

Creating the Right Impression

Young people with problems are frequently in open or repressed conflict with their parents. If the pastor is going to be open for counseling, he cannot identify himself with either parents or young people, but rather must show both that he is capable of objective and sympathetic understanding. The danger is that he will fall into the traditional parental approach to young people by assuming that all is well between them and their parents. In a benevolent and lighthearted way, perhaps, he throws his weight behind the parental side by repeating the timeworn clichés and shallow advice that go along with the

49

bankrupt philosophy that telling young people what to do is the way to get them to do it. More often it is the way to create resistance. Young people will not come to him for counsel if they feel his role as pastor commits him to the opposing side, for he would not understand their position. He gives the impression that he is reprimanding, even in a patronizing kindliness, the youth who are disruptive with their elders.

The pastor is often drawn into this unfortunate position by the parents who ask him to speak to their youngster because they can "no longer do anything with him." So the pastor feels he must approach the youth on behalf of his parents. It is only natural that he meets the same indifference as do they. The pastor is simply trying to be co-operative, and in this respect he is to be commended. On the other hand, the factors involved in these instances which the parents are not always able to see make it advisable for him to rely on his own judgment. The parents may have used the commandment "Honour thy father and thy mother" as a club, so that the young person already feels that the authorities in religion are against him. The parents by the same token may feel the pastor is their natural ally in the conflict for the same reason. It would help to structure the situation if the pastor would present the balanced teaching of the Scriptures whenever he refers to family relationships—not only the commandment to the children, but also the admonition to the parents.

I am becoming increasingly impressed by the wisdom of Paul's words: "Ye fathers, provoke not your children to wrath." Over one third of the total number of young people with whom I counseled in the preceding year had problems that included a violent resentment against one or both parents. Such resentment also creates a violent guilt over it and ultimately leads to a state of inner anxiety. These youth need first to face their real feelings, often repressed, concerning their parents before they will be able to cope with their problem. In this manner they grow to understand both their own and their parents' role in these clashes, and, subsequently, to accept (forgive) themselves and their parents.

If the pastor shows that he understands the two-sidedness of these conflicts, he will be refreshingly different to his youth. They will feel he understands them, as he withholds his own judgments in favor of taking an interest in their opinions. This helps to build up their confidence, since it is an approach that shows confidence in them. It is also the best way to help the parents. In the last analysis parents know they need the help of a pastor who has the confidence of the young people. They will come to him more as counselor than as an ally. In this way he will be able to help them see their own role in the conflict more objectively so that they can take steps to improve it.

Working with young people can be very exasperating. Theirs is a time of emotional upheaval that predisposes them to irresponsibility and disruptiveness and even to explorations into sin. Only as an elder realizes that these are the symptoms of the need for the security of being loved, can he exercise the patience that is needed to carry them over this turbulent period. Because parents are emotionally involved in these conflicts, it is difficult for them to have this patience. The pastor is in a unique position to help out in this situation by supplying the sympathetic understanding that is needed to turn the hearts of the children to the parents and the parents to the children.

Even as there is a danger that the pastor will identify himself with the parents, so there is the opposite extreme that he will identify himself with the youth. Those who err in this direction become so much like "the kids" that they lose their respect. This danger usually centers around the pastor's idea of humor. In his attempt to be popular with the young people, his levity may become suggestive on the one hand or downright silly on the other. If the pastor becomes adolescent in his behavior, he will be competing with his young people rather than helping them. While they want him to show an understanding of their level, they do not want him to be on their level.

There is a need and place for levity. There is also a knack for good humor, and not every pastor has it. If there is any danger that the pastor's sense of being funny would tend to degrade him in the eyes of his young people, he would enhance his counseling possibilities by restraining himself, even though this means that he take a more passive role in the merrymaking. Pastors who are not by nature "lives of the party" or star athletes may feel inadequate as youth pastors. While it may seem that these abilities are an asset at parties and picnics, they do not determine whether young people will confide in him. Youth are far more attracted by the pastor's ability to appreciate their performance than by his ability to perform.

Young people follow the social pattern of their group. Respect for the pastor catches on quickly. Their familiar phrase, "They're all doing it," is not always over matters in good taste, but it can be used to good advantage in regard to the pastor's counseling. Once it gets around that going to the pastor with one's problems is the thing to do, the pastor's education program with his young people is over its big hurdle.

If we pastors could be successful in bringing our counseling ministry to our youth, we would break the barriers to pastoral counseling in one generation. For these are the people who train the generations of tomorrow. Pastoral counseling in the church of today is a movement, and like any other movement it depends upon capturing the youth for its success and its future. The pastor may not stay in his congregation long enough to see these far-reaching results in being successful with his youth, but he can have the satisfaction that his successor will reap the benefits. The Kingdom has been advanced, and this is all that matters.

CHAPTER FIVE

When They Don't Come

PASTOR, GEORGE CRANE IS IN A BAD WAY. I THINK HE SHOULD have a talk with you."

The speaker was Henry Sandberg, an elder on the church council. "What seems to be his trouble?" the pastor asked.

"He's been hitting the bottle pretty hard. His wife tells me he gets depressed—talks of doing away with himself."

The pastor frowned. "Well, how do you suggest I approach him? George isn't the easiest man to talk to, you know. He may even resent it."

Sandberg rubbed his chin. "Yes, that's true. Golly, I don't know what to tell you, Pastor. But I know he needs help. If you do look him up, please don't say anything about who told you. I—I wouldn't want him to know. You understand."

Yes, the pastor understands! But what should he do? There is nothing more disturbing to him than to know that certain people within his congregation are in need of help, but are not coming for it. Should he go to them? Or should he hold back in the hope that they will come to him?

The Role of the Informer

Those who inform the pastor of people who are in need of counseling should be commended for their concern. They should also be encouraged to retain some responsibility for these people and not be content to dump the whole problem in the pastor's lap—with a request for anonymity, at that. This puts the pastor in a most awkward position where he is requested to approach an individual about his problem and incur his resentment by remaining secretive about how he knows about these things. There are times when this secrecy is both wise and necessary. There are also times when it is simply the avoidance of responsibility. This is particularly true in family situations—husbands concerning wive, wives concerning husbands, and parents concerning their children—when one asks the pastor to talk to the offender, expecting this talk to produce a miracle, yet hamstrings him with a limitation like "a little birdie told me."

As we have noted, it is always conducive to better results if the individual with the problem takes the initiative to come to the pastor rather than the pastor's having to accost him. The pastor can often use the informer for this purpose. "Do you suppose," he may say, "that you could persuade *so-and-so* to come to see me? I'll be in my office tomorrow evening. You try your best to get him in here. It would be much better this way." It is surprising how often this will succeed when people actually try.

The pastor needs to evaluate both his information and the one who informs him. The person who tells him about the problem of another and urges him to do something about it may be subconsciously exaggerating it because of his own emotional involvement. The pastor also may become emotionally involved. Worry is contagious, particularly when one has a stake in the problem. The pastor easily becomes perturbed because he feels the situation is in part a reflection on his own role as shepherd of his flock and also because the weight of responsibility is being laid upon him for correcting the situation. As a result he experiences the rise of the destructive emotions of both guilt and anxiety within him. The more a pastor thinks about his own responsibility when he hears about these things, the more the problem becomes his own. This interferes with an objective analysis of the situation.

Many times things are not so bad as the story had it. While it is often true that where there is smoke there is fire, it is often also true that the fire is a small one. Sometimes things have a way of working out by themselves. The small fires are usually under control. They can be fanned into dangerous proportions, however, by the stormy interference of other people. There is need for a pause between the pastor's initial disturbance created by the report and his intrusion into the fray.

Despite this caution the pastor can still go into immediate action. The informer is before him. He may be a disinterested person so far as the problem is concerned. On the other hand, he may be a part of it. In some instances the pastor knows which is the case from the beginning; in others only the continued self-expression of the informer will tell. If the pastor encourages this self-expression by using the counseling approach of responsive listening with the informer, he may find himself already at work on the problem. Some people even use the problems of others as a means of approaching the pastor with their own problems. Hesitant over telling him their problems, they use the problems of others as ways of easing themselves into the counselee role. The "trial balloon" furnishes them with the encouragement they need concerning the pastor's attitude and approach.

When Mrs. Garfield came to her pastor to ask his help with her husband, she gave the impression that he was the problem. "I can't do anything with him. He won't go to church; he won't listen to reason. He has no consideration—all he wants is his own satisfaction. I tell you, I can hardly stand to live with him any more. He'll have me in a nervous breakdown. I hate to say this, but he's struck me on several occasions."

Immediately the pastor feels anger rising within him at such a brute, who treats his wife so harshly, who won't even go to church. If he could just have a talk with him, maybe he could straighten him out. Counseling with Mr. Garfield, then, becomes the obvious solution to the problem. Counseling with

Mr. Garfield, however, is a long way from happening. In the meantime he has Mrs. Garfield. In spite of the fact that the problem seems to be with Mr. Garfield, counseling with his wife may be of great help. The chances are that through the counseling process she will begin to see her own responsibility in the problem and ways in which she can improve her role as wife. This does not mean that Mr. Garfield is not primarily responsible for the problem; it does mean that the problems between individuals usually have two sides, and that any improvement on either side will usually have a good effect on the other.

When all efforts to get the problemed person into the pastor's office fail, including the efforts of the informer, the pastor may still counsel with the person through the informer. This is particularly true when the informer has an opening with the person which the pastor feels he lacks. I have discovered that quite inadvertently I have been training student counselors in this manner. These are the students who have received help in counseling and are using what they have learned in an effort to reach those students who need counseling but who are reluctant to seek the pastor's help. They are also the informers who get pointers from me concerning the counseling approach and who return at intervals to report their progress and to discuss future procedure.

Not Suffered Enough

The reason why some of the individuals within the congregation who need help do not come to the pastor is that they have not suffered enough as yet. Until the situation becomes intolerable, many people will continue to struggle on alone with their problems. It takes an intense amount of pain to overcome the resistance of their pride and to force them to face up to the realities of the situation. The prodigal son needed help long before he was aware of it himself. He needed counsel when he was dissatisfied in his home. However, he thought he knew the answer: he would demand his share of the inheritance and leave the farm for the city. He would escape.

Anybody who knew him and was interested in his welfare when he was wasting his substance in riotous living might have told the local rabbi about him in the hope that he could help him. But it is doubtful if the prodigal would have listened to anybody. Even when his money was gone and his friends turned him down, he was unapproachable. He could get a job. But when he was reduced to feeding the despised swine, his pride was gone, and when he would have eaten even the husks that the swine ate but no man gave unto him, he was desperate. Then it was that he "came to himself." Now he would go to his father for help—but even then not as a son but as a hired hand.

Even people who have been to the pastor before and received his help may hesitate to return if they fall back into their trouble. It is humiliating for them to have to tell the pastor they are having difficulties again when they have previously told him all was going along fine. The pastor may help to create this block by showing too much joy over the good that his counselee reports, so that the counselee hesitates to disappoint him. Often the pastor does so as an encouragement to his counselee and does not realize the predicament he is putting him in should the report later have to be reversed. The counselee may rather tell him what he thinks he wants to hear.

The pastor often complains that his people do not come to him with their problems until things are "in a mess." Yet it is this progress into the mess that at times creates the desperation that makes the counselee amenable for help—without this desperation he may not be able to come or able to receive. The counselee himself often confesses: "I know I should have come to you sooner—but—well, I thought I could handle things by myself—yet I see now that I can't. Besides, those steps up to your office can seem awfully high."

Alcoholics Anonymous insist that an alcoholic be in this state of desperation before they will take up his case. It is as the alcoholic mentally "hits the bottom" that he realizes he must quit his drinking or lose everything, and that by himself he is defeated. He must both want to quit and want help. Sometimes this state of mind can be precipitated by the approach of a friend, so that the individual is brought to the awareness of his need before he hits this bottom. In the case of the alcoholic it could be a member of Alcoholics Anonymous. In the case of problemed people as a whole it could be the pastor of the church.

Going to Them

After his attempts to get the individual who has been referred to him to come on his own have been given sufficient time to materialize, or as much time as the pastor feels he dare give, and the individual has not come, the pastor may feel he should go to him. His shepherd heart goes out to the one sheep that is lost more than over the ninety and nine that seem secure, and he feels constrained to make contact. When this individual's problem is centered in his own suffering, the approach is rather easily made. Those who are bogged down in worry, depressed over social, family, or vocational failures, tormented with inner fears and anxieties, are often relieved when the pastor breaks the ice. What little resistance he encounters is usually initial embarrassment. Without apology he can approach such people by saying, "I understand you are having some difficulties, and I was wondering if I could be of some help. Would you like to talk to me about things?"

The pastor will find that the percentage of positive responses to such a query is extremely high. The individual may be taken momentarily aback and stammer out something like, "Oh, I don't know. It's nothing much. I wouldn't know what to say. I don't know if it would do any good or not." To this the pastor can reply, "Perhaps it would help. Would you like to make an appointment when we can get together?" By this time the person usually has recovered from his shock and says, "Well, maybe so." If, however, the unusual happens and he says flatly, "No, I don't think so," there is little the pastor can do but accept this decision. He may simply reply, "That's perfectly all right. It's entirely up to you. If you ever do feel you would like to see me, don't hesitate to call."

When the problem concerns a violation of Christian morality, the task is more difficult. When individuals are involved in immorality, drunkenness, financial irregularities, or the like, they usually feel guilty—particularly if they are connected with the church. The pastor is automatically identified with their conscience, which they may be trying hard to talk down. When he approaches them, they may express resentment. Because they must work hard to keep their defenses intact, they may speak boldly and arrogantly to him, justifying their position by rationalizations and defending themselves on the basis of their own code, which says there is nothing wrong with what they are doing. Or they may angrily deny that there is anything to what the pastor has indicated. "I can take care of myself," they tell him, "and I don't care to associate with those gossips of the church with their holier-than-thou fronts." Or they may take the opposite position and clam up, even to the point of rudeness.

In either case the reaction is caused by guilt and leads to more guilt. Often these individuals experience genuine regret for their behavior after the emotions of the incident subside. This shame may prevent their contacts with the pastor even if they change their mind about seeing him. So we can see the danger involved when the pastor starts out to talk to those whose problem is showing itself in open sin. It is for this reason that the pastor may "stew" a great deal before he makes the contact and even then may leave without bringing the matter up.

Pastor Johnson was told about one of his young people who was pregnant out of wedlock. He was afraid to approach the girl directly, because he was also told that she was defending herself on the grounds of simply putting on weight and that she might demand to know who told him. So instead he decided to call at the girl's home, figuring that either the girl or her parents would know why he was there and would bring the subject up. They conversed about everything from the weather to politics for over two hours, but no one ever hinted that there was a problem. So he left somewhat confused over what he should do next. Within two weeks the pregnancy became public knowledge. The family also found out that the pastor had known all along. This time when he called on them, they blamed him bitterly for not telling them. "I thought you knew," he said. "That's why I called that evening." But in the sting of their humiliation they needed a scapegoat, and the pastor was it.

If the pastor has the opportunity to meet on other matters with an individual who is having difficulties, he may succeed in getting him to relate his problem by being alert to respond to whatever clues are given. Even without this ready-made contact he may achieve similar results by simply calling upon him at his house. Yet if the matter is pressing, and the person may suspect the purpose of the call, it is better to come to the point. To speak frankly in matters such as these requires the support of a relationship of rapport. The advantages that the pastor has taken to cultivate this rapport in his previous contacts with the individual may be the decisive factor in his success at this time. Whatever effort he puts forth to know and understand his people is an investment in his future ministry to them. Once rapport has been established, indirect methods of getting to the point may miss the mark entirely. Not only are they time-consuming for both the pastor and the parishioner, but they may smack of duplicity to the parishioner who sees through them.

If there has been no opportunity to establish rapport beforehand, the pastor may still create a support for his inquiry by his manner of approach. As we have noted, the danger in such an inquiry is the creation of resentment within the individual. Whatever would keep this resentment to a minimum would be the best approach. We have the pattern for such an approach in Paul's Letter to the Galatians: "Brethren, if a man is overtaken in any trespass, you who are spiritual should restore him in a spirit of gentleness. Look to yourself, lest you too be tempted" (6:1, R.S.V.).

It is this spirit of gentleness as it is conveyed in words and countenance that disarms the person. The absence of a *judgmental* attitude, the presence of humility, takes the person off the defensive. Even with this approach the pastor may encounter initial resentment. If he can bear with the individual, he can often "weather the storm," and the results are an adequate reward for his patience. As he continues to talk and listen in the same gentle spirit, the resentment may gradually wear off, and before the interview comes to a close the person may change his mind about the pastor's offer of help.

Mrs. George Sanderson had on several occasions called the pastor in a state of near hysteria over her marital problems. Each time she had presented what appeared to be evidences of her husband's infidelity. Since she was nearing her breaking point, the pastor felt he should try to have a talk with Mr. Sanderson. This would not be easy, because Mr. Sanderson was not a member of the church, and the pastor had had only casual contacts with him. Mrs. Sanderson agreed that the pastor should talk to her husband and that he could tell him that she had come to him for counsel. The pastor realized that it was necessary to protect the man's ego in his approach to him. He planned his visit when Mr. Sanderson was alone, and after a minimum of introductory talk began as follows:

P. I hope you will not misunderstand what I have to say, Mr. Sanderson. Believe me, I am saying it only because I think you should know and because I want to be of any help I can. Mrs. Sanderson has talked to me. She's quite upset. I suppose you know what about.

S. (flushing) She imagines a lot of things. She's just excitable, that's all.

P. I see. I hope you won't hold it against her that she talked with me. She was trying to get help for the situation.

S. Well, I wish she would have told me.

P. Sure, I know. I want you to understand that I am only here to help.

S. Well, I don't know what can be done. I don't have much time to spend at home. My work demands me at all hours.

P. I suppose maybe this is one of the things that makes it hard for her.

S. Oh, sure. She doesn't like it. But what can I do? I won't jeopardize my job.

P. That is, you feel there is no way you can work it to be at home more.

S. I don't see how. (He went on to give examples of his work demands.)

Mr. Sanderson was becoming more relaxed all the time. He was beginning to see that although his wife had talked to the pastor, he was not allying himself with her against him. In a short time he was able to collect his thoughts and come to a decision.

S. Tell you what, Reverend. I'll have a talk with her. Like I said, she imagines things. She hasn't been too well lately. I'll give you a ring near the end of the week, and we'll be having you over.

P. All right. And I appreciate your spirit.

S. Uh—yeah—thanks for coming around, Reverend.

The pastor never received the call. But he learned from Mrs. Sanderson that things had really changed. Whether she had been right in her accusations the pastor may never know, but it was evident that Mr. Sanderson had been guilty at least of neglect and that the pastor's call had brought this forcibly to his attention. If he was guilty of more, the shock of the call may have brought him to his senses and his conscience.

Besides being a counselor the pastor is the prophet who pronounces God's judgment upon sin. When does he speak as this prophet of the Lord to the errant parishioner? Although the pastor may feel constrained to warn the offender so that "his blood will be upon his own head," there is something more important than having the satisfaction that he has discharged his responsibility. The pastor's first consideration is to win the brother. So long as he can keep the door open to the sinner, there is the possibility that he may enter. The prophetic "Thus saith the Lord!" may stiffen the resistance, or it may crack it wide open. It is a make-or-break proposition. One may get through to the sinner sooner by reflecting his feelings in a counseling approach. Only when all attempts to reach the person by less drastic means have been tried should the pastor resort to the prophetic warning. Those who will not hear the gospel must hear the law. The prophetic warning can be compared to an operation that the physician may undertake only when the more natural methods to help the patient have failed.

"Of some have compassion, making a difference: and others save with fear, pulling them out of the fire; hating even the garment spotted by the flesh." (Jude 22-23.)

In Conclusion

In these situations where "they don't come," the pastor is torn inwardly between waiting too long and getting in too fast. His own emotionally disturbed ego adds to the tension. Before he can decide what to do, he must keep his own problem out of it, so that he will have an open mind for the Holy Spirit to direct. This kind of objectivity begins in the practice of intercessory prayer. But even intercessory prayer can become self-centered if precautions are not taken to counteract its doing so. The pastor can guard against this danger by keeping the person's need and his own role separate in the structure of his prayer. We should pray first for the person who has the problem as though the Lord had no intention of using us to counsel him. This helps to make it a genuinely intercessory prayer. Secondly, we should pray for our own role as pastor, so that if it is God's plan to use us to meet this person's need, we will be receptive to God's guidance. When the pastor can put his trust in the transcendent guidance of God, he can evaluate the situation without the subjective interference of guilt and fear.

There is no rule that can be used for all cases when entities as varied as human personalities are involved. Nor can there be such a rule where there is a higher Guidance for the ministry than the minister's own mind. God can be literally *ruled* out. The pastor is not in this business alone; he is working for the higher Counselor. It is he who works in us, through us, beyond us, and in spite of us, "to will and to do of his good pleasure." The apostle Paul could evaluate his work without either honest conceit or false modesty because he saw it all in terms of the grace of God. "But by the grace of God I am what I am: and his grace which was bestowed upon me was not in vain; but I laboured more abundantly than they all: yet not I, but the grace of God which was with me." (I Cor. 15:10.)

It is this grace that the pastor takes into account when he faces his problems with those who do not come. Trusting in God, rather than causing the pastor to do less, frees him to do more.

CHAPTER SIX

Preaching and Counseling

IN THE APOLOGY TO THE AUGSBURG CONFESSION THE CREDIT FOR the large attendance at the church services in the Reformation Era is given to the quality of the preaching. "For the audiences are held by useful and clear sermons. . . . The true adornment of the churches is godly, useful and clear doctrine." Luther himself was an example of this type of preaching. Even before the Reformation he was so popular as a preacher at the city church that the people demanded to hear him once a day.

Both preaching and counseling are concerned with the problems of people. Neither is subservient to the other. Sermons have given the solution to the problems of many people. They have also served to draw to the preacher those whose problems needed individual attention. Usually it is the sermon that helps people in their problems that also draws them to the pastor. How then can the pastor use his sermon as a companion ministry with his counseling?

I faced this problem in the parish ministry; I face it even more as a college chaplain. To establish a voluntary counseling service at a school where it had not existed previously meant that I needed to gain the confidence of the students. Teaching in the classroom was a great help. College chapel also offered me an excellent opportunity: I could preach to them. The sermon that moves people to come to the pastor with their problems is the sermon that comes to grips with these problems. When his preaching is helpful to them, they feel encouraged to come to him for counseling. What then can we say are the essential characteristics of this kind of preaching?

Theological Stability

From early times congregations have confessed their faith as a part of the church service. The confession of faith evolved through the centuries as people felt the need for greater clarity in their religious beliefs. Our three ecumenical creeds were the result of this need. The simple statement "Jesus is Lord," which was apparently the earliest expression of Christian faith, was superseded by these other creeds, not with the idea of changing it but of expanding it to meet the need of a growing church for a more definitive position. The Apostles' Creed evolved from the Old Roman Symbol, which was used as a baptismal confession in the first centuries. When a controversy arose over the nature of the person of Christ, the early creed proved to be inadequate in its coverage, and the Nicene and Athanasian creeds were formulated to express the thinking of the church on this doctrine. There is a psychological need for theology; it satisfies the demand of the intellect for a definite structure in ideas and is reason's way of grasping religion.

Theology need not imply a technical theological terminology, nor complicated doctrinal minutiae, nor an unreasonable, narrow-minded dogmatism. The psychological need for theology is the need for explicit expression in regard to the fundamentals of belief. The preacher who is consistently vague in his theology is neglecting the need of his people for a faith that can be defined. Any reference to theology by the preacher is often accompanied by an apology—as though both he and his hearers viewed definiteness in religious matters as a homiletical hindrance. "The beautiful isle of somewhere" finds its modern counterpart in the dreamy theology of somehow. The preacher says that he feels that somehow what he says is true and that somehow what he thinks will happen, will happen. So far as any theology of "how" is concerned, the preacher gives the impression that this does not really matter—what difference does it make?

The omission of theology from the sermon may be the result of a conflict in the preacher's mind. His seminary training may have removed him from the religious beliefs of his congregation, and he may be reluctant to bring these differences to the attention of his people—particularly since their beliefs are usually more in line with the historical doctrinal position, as well as the present confessional adherence, of his denomination. He may evade the issue entirely or try to conceal it behind carefully chosen words from which each may draw his own interpretation. Or he may use the theological, confessional, or biblical phrases but in his own mind be aware he is interpreting these phrases differently than his people. The difficulty with this elastic use of words is that ultimately it destroys the purpose of words— namely, to convey the thought of the speaker to the listener. This is a day of the liberal conservative and the conservative liberal. There is a dread of sounding too orthodox and a dread of sounding too liberal, and this middle-of-the-road fetish is working havoc with our doctrinal preaching. The preacher feels constrained to word his sermon so that he arouses no criticism from the wing he desires to be associated with and yet is not too offensive to those of the other wing either.

People who listen to preaching of this kind for very long will suspect the truth. If they have problems, they will be even more disturbed. Anything that makes them dubious concerning their pastor's beliefs undermines their confidence in their own. Of course, a pastor can scarcely preach what he does not believe; yet this preaching in a theological vacuum is leaving unsatisfied the hunger of the human mind for a spiritual credo. Since the theology of the church is pertinent to pastoral counseling, its inclusion in the sermon would have this same relevance to the people in the pew.

Understanding of Human Nature

The rapport that is needed in counseling can be initiated in the pulpit if the sermons show an understanding of human nature. Before he can understand his people, the preacher must understand himself. This is an even more difficult task in the ministerial role than otherwise. People consider the preacher a professional example of Christian living. He may become so used to this picture of himself that he tends to rationalize or ignore anything about himself that is counter to it. He is even supposed to be above having the troublesome problems of his people. The great danger is that he will not acknowledge his problems when he has them, and so will be unable to understand these problems in his people. Naturally his preaching will show this lack of understanding.

People who are going to help others with their problems had better begin at home. Before a psychoanalyst is ready to practice, he must himself undergo an analysis. A minister of the church ought to be no less thorough in his preparation. It may be a profitable venture for theological seminaries to encourage their students to experience pastoral counseling in their problem areas as a prerequisite for the pastoral-counseling ministry. As one ministerial student said, "I have come for counseling because I have a few things that are bothering me, and I can't expect to counsel with others if I cannot handle my own problems." If the preacher faces his problems in his personality, in his faith, and in his family, his thoughts will naturally go to these problems as he seeks to apply his text. His preaching will show he understands from personal experience. Because it was applied first to himself, his sermon will "ring a bell" in the minds of his hearers. The Bible itself is a source book in human nature. The preacher who is a conscientious student of the Scriptures should learn much about people, including himself. He will also have an abundance of material upon which to base his sermons. The study of psychology will also help him to understand people. If he gains from science a knowledge of the *modus operandi* of the human personality, he can learn to recognize these patterns in himself and others. In this manner he will grow sensitive to the psychological clues that interpret human behavior, and will be able to explain the intricacies of human nature to his people. (Let him beware of using a psychological vocabulary; congregations want a pastor, not a psychologist.)

The sermons that draw people for counseling are the sermons that show people the pastor knows how they feel. As he wrestles with the destructive emotions within his own breast—his doubts, his ego disturbances, his anxieties, his resentments—he will find answers to these problems that he can give to others. He will know what is going on within his people because he has faced what goes on within himself. The study of the Scriptures and psychology are more profitable when they are both prompted by and applied to the battle within. Sermons growing out of such deep searchings establish an identity with the hearer that stimulates immediate rapport. "Canned" sermons will not do this simply because they do not emerge out of the struggles of the preacher's own soul. "I had a feeling you were talking directly to me," is the response of the hearer to the preacher whose message rings with a conviction that somebody's else's craftsmanship cannot give him.

Personal Religion

People with problems often come to church to find help from religion. They are most likely to get this help from sermons that are focused on the personal religious life. Sermons on social action—race relations, international ethics, and world relief— are essential to the preaching schedule, but it is the sermon on the religion of the inner life that moves people to ask for counseling. The psychology of religion defines religion as man's response to a Creator of values in which the Creator himself is the supreme value. The person in the pew has a need first of all for God himself. People are the same today as they were several centuries ago when they traveled from all over Europe to talk with Brother Lawrence. When this medieval monk counseled with people on practicing the presence of God, he was satisfying the fundamental need of the soul to which Augustine gave his eloquent testimony: "Our hearts are restless, O God, until they find their rest in thee."

Because the pastor is personally involved in the activities of his church, he may find himself grinding his own ax in his sermons. He feels dependent upon the interest and attendance of the church member for the carrying out of the church's program. Under the strain of keeping this program in progress he is tempted to use his sermon to shame or to club his people into conformity. His emphasis then will be more upon law than upon good news and upon externals rather than motives. The preaching of personal religion depends upon the pastor's ability to hold his vision upon the essentials of the kingdom of God despite the immediate problems of the congregation.

When a person has a problem, his personal religion often suffers. In fact, he may feel he has lost it. This damage to his spiritual life may seem to him to be the cause, rather than the effect, of his problem. This was the way Joe felt. "I am disgusted with myself," he said. "I don't seem to be getting along well at all. I think it is because I need a faith. I used to think I believed in God, but I was too young really to understand." We found that the source of his problem lay in the damage unhappy personal relationships had done to his emotions. His resentment and bitterness over these traumas subconsciously contradicted his belief in God, especially in a God of love.

Carl put it this way: "I'm just miserably unhappy and I worry about everything. I try to pray, but God seems a million miles away. Sometimes—and I hate to say this—I wonder if he even exists. I think if I could get my faith back, I would be all right." The root of his trouble was guilt. He had practiced masturbation

70

and felt defiled in the eyes of God. Unable to face him, he ceased to see him at all.

The preacher moves in a circle where God is taken for granted in a conversational way, and he will have to remind himself that there are doubters among his hearers and that they are often people with problems. In his sermons he should seek to stimulate faith, not only by pointing to authority or giving rational support, but by attempting to alleviate the emotional causes of doubt. His challenge is to preach the love and forgiveness of God (the gospel) in a way that will take effect in the lives of his hearers. Theology shows him this way in the doctrine of the incarnation. In Jesus Christ we have the humanization of the love and forgiveness of God. The life and person of the Master have an appeal all their own. He is *the Word* most likely to penetrate the depths of the troubled personality; he is the tangible one through whom man can know and love God. Even as he touched the inner lives of his hearers and drew them to him for counseling, so the sermon that presents him to the people is in a position to achieve these same effects.

Ring of Sincerity

Once when I had a problem and needed help, I heard Peter Marshall preach. His text was the story of Jesus and the woman who anointed his feet with oil. I left his church feeling much better than when I entered. My help came not only from what he said but also from the sincerity with which he said it. He preached as one who knew God in a personal way. The scribes and Pharisees could quote the authorities of the past with meticulous accuracy, but they had nothing of their own to give. It is from the preacher's own experience in his spiritual life that he learns how to make religion practical to his people. "I believed, and therefore have I spoken."

The pastor's sermons reflect his personal devotional life. The time he spends in communion with God is a blessing not only to himself but also to his people. It is from these periods of meditation and prayer that he is spiritually vitalized to preach with conviction. The man who keeps company with Christ has a radiance that cannot be hidden; his people will sense that a man of God is in the pulpit.

The many demands upon the pastor's time are a threat to his devotional life. So long as he is within reach of a telephone, he cannot call his soul his own. Always fearful lest he offend someone, he may be drawn away from his time with God to matters of less importance. If he neglects his personal devotional life with any consistency, it is like failing to put fuel in a motor: he will begin to run dry.

When there is a dearth in his inner spiritual life, he may try to make up for it by emphasizing religion in an external manner. He may assume an air of sanctimony, but being unnatural in his behavior, he lacks the spontaneity of sincerity. He may become a legalist and take refuge in a religion that can be observed in a set of rules. Even a worthy cause—labor-management relationships or world peace—can become his tangible substitute for a faith in the intangible. Such a cause is worthy of his devotion as a minister of the church; yet it can in no way compensate for a deficiency in his personal relationship with God. The conservative's attack against the liberal and the liberal's attack against social evil may both be symptoms of this deficiency. The more bankrupt a pastor is in his spiritual life, the more violently "anti" he may become in his homiletical efforts. It is from the experience of his relationship with his God that he can preach from the heart to people with problems. Unfortunately for his own morale, he is often unaware of the inspiration he has given to those struggling with defeat.

It is not enough to tell people to have faith or even to describe all the values of faith. What they need is someone who can tell them how to get this faith. Only the pastor who has developed his own faith is in a position to do this. It is not sufficient to warn people against yielding to temptations without telling them how to recognize the subtleties of rationalization and how to

72

resist them when they are recognized. It is the pastor whose knowledge of temptation rests upon his own spiritual battles with temptation who alone can do this. The big weakness of preaching is that the layman is told what to do but not how to do it. People with problems are often aware of what they should do to help themselves, but it is part of their problem that they seem unable to do it. The kind of preaching that meets their need and draws them for counseling is characterized in one layman's appraisal of his pastor: "When our minister talks about God," he said, "you know he is talking about *his* God."

Invitive Attitude

We have analyzed what it is that makes a counselor approachable. There is a similar quality in preaching. Let us call it an invitive attitude. It is a pulpit approach that makes the listener feel at ease in the preacher's presence. It is composed of three ingredients: humility, tolerance, and humanliness.

Humility. I have heard "name" preachers who were obviously aware of their prominence. A preacher does not have to be a name, however, to feel important in the pulpit. To those in the pews before him he is an authority. How can he maintain humility? It is a custom among Lutheran preachers to have Luther's Sacristy Prayer in their own sacristies. Just before they enter the pulpit, they read this prayer:

O Lord God Thou hast made me a pastor and teacher in the Church. Thou seest how unfit I am to administer rightly this great and responsible office; and had I been without Thy aid and counsel I would surely have ruined it long ago. Therefore do I invoke Thee.

Now gladly do I desire to yield and consecrate my heart and mouth to this ministry! I desire to teach the congregation. I too desire ever to learn and to keep Thy Word, my constant companion, and to meditate thereupon earnestly.

Use me as Thy instrument in Thy service. Only do not Thou forsake me, for if I am left to myself, I will certainly bring it all to destruction. Amen.

While a prayer of this nature may help to inspire humility, its continual use may become a form that boomerangs. The preacher may use it as a preparatory ritual to stimulate a few pious thoughts so that he can see himself as a hero in humility. A little honest reflection will bring to his mind his own shortcomings and limitations—including his pride—which will move him to depend upon God for the efficacy of his preaching. His challenge is to lead people to the attitude of mind where Christ and they can meet. This is a humble task, for as in counseling so in preaching, he must decrease while the Lord must increase.

Tolerance. Tolerance is an attitude toward people rather than an attitude toward evil. The preacher must condemn sin; yet he must love the sinner. In fact, as C. S. Lewis points out, the reason he hates sin is that he loves the man who sins.[1] Jesus himself is an illustration of this tolerance. Although he strongly disapproved of adultery, he said to the adulteress thrown at his feet by the intolerant Pharisees, "Neither do I condemn thee: go, and sin no more." This tolerance in preaching must extend also to those outside the congregation. A harsh and condemning attitude, no matter to whom it is directed, is a barrier to counseling. People often feel that their own problems are a reflection on their character, and they will see in any intolerance on the part of the preacher a frightening possibility that he might also condemn them. The preacher must preach the law as well as the gospel. It is the spirit in which he preaches the law that is important for counseling. If he gets the slightest pleasure out of denouncing people for their sins, he is probably not spiritually fit to do the job. But if he has the genuine sorrow over sin of the prophet of the Lord, his preaching of the law will not show the intolerance that it might if his personal resentments were abetting the cause. There is no conflict between the ethical role of the preacher as prophet and his permissive role as counselor so long as his motive for both is love and so long as he does not

[1] *Christian Behavior* (New York: The Macmillan Co., 1943), p. 40.

confuse the two. People expect and accept the prophet of righteousness in the pulpit, but they do not expect him to preach in
the counseling room, any more than they would expect him to
preach in the classroom. By agitating the presence of guilt within
the sinner, prophetic preaching of the law may be the means
for bringing people to the pastor for confession.

Humanliness. Although the preacher is a man of wisdom, he
can sound too wise. As good as he is supposed to be, he can give
the impression of being too good. If his preaching gives his
people the impression that he is a fellow who could win any
argument, whose emotions are always under his control, whose
adjustment to life is close to perfect, they may feel he is beyond
the feelings of their infirmities. Their ever-present feelings of
inferiority will be accentuated, and they may feel too inadequate
even to approach him. Too often laymen have thought of the
preacher as a superearthly sort of creature whose interests and
feelings are foreign to theirs. Sermons that stimulate rapport
show the preacher as he really is—a human being, "a man of like
passions as we are."

Preaching has its oratorical barriers to an invitive attitude.
The pulpit tone can repel people because it is unnatural. Shout
ing helps the emphasis, but it is usually associated with anger
and is also frightening. Anything decidedly beyond the bounds
of the conversational pattern, even ornate and dramatic wording,
can dampen the desire to confide. The preacher is sharing with
his people his insights into an understanding of the mind and
purposes of God. He is not preaching *at* them. His sermon
should move them to say, "I think I could talk to a man like
that." By talking to the individual rather than to the audience,
he will prepare the way for the individual's approach to him
rather than discourage it.

The pastor as a preacher and the pastor as a counselor work
together to meet the needs of people. Preaching is not adapted
to minister to individual needs as is the interchange of conversation in the counseling relationship. Nor can it always reach the

more serious and deep-seated problems. On the other hand, counseling is too time-consuming to be a means for ministering to all the problemed people of the parish. The preaching ministry is also a means for the prevention of problems. For those whose problems require individual attention it is the needed introduction to the counselor and what he has to offer. The counseling ministry in turn gives the pastor excellent material for his sermons. Naturally he dare not use his counseling cases as illustrations, but the emotional pattern of people with problems is indicative of the way people in general are adjusting to life. Even as the mentally ill experience in the extreme what normal people experience in varying degrees, so the people with problems in a congregation are experiencing in the extreme what the rest of the members are experiencing in varying degrees. If the preacher's sermons reflect his awareness of these emotional patterns, his preaching will be on a level with the needs of his people. The same can be said for his prayers and for the manner in which he conducts the entire worship service. Preaching and counseling are dependent upon each other for an effective ministry to people with problems.

CHAPTER SEVEN

Calling and Counseling

CALLING IS ONE OF THE FIRST AREAS OF THE PASTOR'S TASK THAT he neglects when he becomes pressed for time. This is not necessarily because he minimizes its importance but rather because, excluding the ministry to the seriously ill, calling has no time schedule which must be met. The sermon has to be delivered on Sunday morning; the council meeting is at 8 P.M. on Tuesday; the parish paper has its deadline; the funerals and weddings are at appointed hours. Even the counseling program is scheduled in that appointments are requested and office hours are respected. Calling can be put off until we have time to get at it. As a result the pastor rarely gets caught up in his calling. Finding a solution to the busyness of a minister's schedule is a problem in itself, and we shall take it up in a later chapter. The layman feels this neglect of calling a serious shortcoming. "Pastor Blank is a fine fellow," he will tell his neighbor. "He preaches good sermons. But he doesn't call on his people like his should." To which his neighbor will often reply, "Our minister is the same way. He has been here two years now and has never been in our house yet."

The Need for Calling

Before a Methodist minister is received into full membership in his conference, he must answer publicly a set of questions which were originally drawn up by John Wesley, one of which is, "Will you visit from house to house?" The founders and leaders of the denomination insisted upon this house-to-house visitation as one of the major functions of the ministry because they realized its importance. The calling ministry takes the pastor into the home. To many families this is a manifestation of his interest in them. The home front is often the battleground for serious conflicts. When the pastor is at this strategic spot, he may often find that his calling ministry is an extension of his counseling ministry. A home that appears to be ideal to an outsider may be far from ideal to those on the inside. As one young lady said, "My family is a house divided against itself. Yet everybody around us thinks we are such a wonderful family. Sort of ironical, isn't it!"

Often a person feels he would like to talk with his pastor, but he keeps putting it off. When he *does* come, his problem is usually much worse. What pastor has not felt like saying to his counselee, "Why, oh, why didn't you come to see me sooner— before things got into such straits!" When the pastor calls on such an individual, however, the obstacles that led him to procrastinate are partially removed. The presence of his pastor before him in his own home is an influence to move him to act. He may come to the point "Say, Pastor, sometime when you are not too busy, I'd like to talk with you." The calling program provides the counseling ministry with its cutting edge. From sixty to eighty per cent of a pastor's counseling may be done in his calling until his counseling program is established.

The pastor's call, like his sermon, tells a great deal about the pastor. The picture of himself that he provides his parishioner during his call may be the deciding factor in the parishioner's coming to him for counseling. His call is therefore a pump primer in relationship to his counseling program. It is a preview of his counseling. The layman needs this preview, and consequently the pastor should call. There is, however, nothing automatic in the efficacy of a calling program. The purpose of a preview is to encourage people to desire the real thing, but not all previews accomplish their purpose. The quality of the call is as important as the call.

Effective Calling

In contrast to preaching, calling, like counseling, is personal work or in many cases family work. Although the house-to-house call may readily turn into counseling, we usually think of it as a less specific type of conversation. In his calling the pastor is a conversationalist. A good conversationalist is not to be confused with a good talker. The person who can speak at length and in an interesting way is an entertainer. He performs and others are the audience. Conversation, on the other hand, is a give-and-take arrangement in which all parties participate in the talking. A good conversationalist is one who stimulates others to contribute to the conversation; he treats as important whatever they want to talk about and shows an interest in what they say; he is above all a good listener. People find him easy to talk to because he respects their opinions, and stimulating because he also has opinions of his own. The pastor as a conversationalist therefore is not essentially different from the pastor as a counselor: the principles of counseling are fundamental also to the art of good conversation. Because of this the conversation in calling is a natural introduction to the counseling approach; it indicates to the parishioner the ease in which his problem could be discussed, should he bring it up.

If a troubled person talks long enough to a responsive listener, his resistance will lessen; and without his realizing it, his conversation will become increasingly personal until he begins to drop the hints of his problem that the alert pastor will follow up. Even on the telephone the pastor may pick up these clues. Pastor Robinson happened to call Mrs. Brunson to ask her about her work in the ladies' society. After about five minutes of conversation upon this matter Mrs. Brunson said, "I haven't been able to do this job as I would like—there have been a few complications." The pastor responded to this statement in a way that led her to say, "Things haven't been going so good of late." Before he hung up, Pastor Robinson had made an appointment to call on Mrs. Brunson. He was surprised to learn that the Brunsons were on the verge of separating, and he had never suspected it, nor had they intended to talk to him about it. The phone call was the beginning of a counseling ministry that saved a home. Of course, it could scarcely have happened on a rural party line.

The kind of calling that is in line with the counseling approach demands of the pastor a wide and spontaneous interest in all of life. People differ in the things over which they are primarily concerned. Some like to talk about religion, others about health, others their work and hobbies, or their home and children; still others like to talk about politics, music, art and drama, sports, or economics. The pastor cannot afford to appear condescending or unsympathetic toward any of these things, since they are the entrance way into the person himself. People interpret the pastor's interest in their interests as an interest in *them*, since a person's interests are inseparable from the person. Although it helps to know something about these various interests of people, the pastor can show his interest simply by his desire to learn. This puts the parishioner into a position of authority, which he naturally enjoys. Also the pastor profits personally from the call: he learns something. His calling program is an education toward his ministry. The more he learns about the interests of people, the more he can share their life and apply religion to it.

The pastoral call also needs a time structure. When should the pastor make his house-to-house visit, and how long should he stay? The chances are usually better for finding the entire family at home in the evening than in the afternoon. Again the pastor has to resist the pressure of too many evening meetings so that there is time each week to call upon the families and breadwinners. From a counseling standpoint the afternoon call has an advantage also in that the housewife is often home alone, and a call upon one individual is more likely to turn into a counseling interview than a call upon a family.

While calling by appointment is timesaving for the pastor, there are also advantages in calling unannounced. People can be prepared for the pastor's call to the point of artificiality or even resistance. Although the conditions and conversation of the call are likely to be more natural and spontaneous when he calls unannounced, the pastor should remember that he is interrupting the plans and schedule of these people. Let him be considerate and not prolong his call to the point where the interruption could cause frustration and inconvenience. Most people, even in our twentieth-century pace, can spare a half hour. If the call should turn into counseling, however, more than this amount of time is needed. This raises another problem, which will be discussed later in the chapter.

Alert for the Symptoms

When the pastor meets his appointments for counseling, he is prepared for problems and alert to their symptoms. When he visits his members or prospective members, he is prepared for a conversational call. Yet anything can happen. I remember calling upon a very respectable, well-to-do family who were considering membership in the church. To my confusion, I found the lady of the house in a state of semi-intoxication. Not knowing what to do, I followed the old principle of doing nothing I conversed with her with as much composure as I could muster and tried to conclude the visit as normally as possible. From that time forth I was alert for trouble in this family, and I did not have to wait long before an occasion presented itself for counseling.

Most of the clues to problems that the pastor observes in his calling are much less obvious than intoxication. If he takes for granted that all is well, his ears may be insensitive to the allusions that are made to negative feelings. In his assumption that everything is normal he may unconsciously overlook the symptoms of problems and be oblivious to hints that all is *not* well.

One evening when I was feeling successful because I had already completed four calls, I dropped in on a young couple who I had married the previous year. We had what I thought was a gay visit as we laughed and joked about the experiences of the first year of married life. A week later the wife called for an appointment. "I suppose you know what I am here for," she said on arriving.

"No," I said, "I don't believe I do."

"Surely you noticed things were not right when you called the other night," she said. I had to admit that I had not. "Oh, I thought it was obvious. Joe came home from work that night and he had been drinking as usual. We had a big fight. You caught us right in the middle of it. Our marriage is breaking up. I don't know if anything can be done or not, but I have to talk to somebody about it or I will lose my mind." I was hit between the eyes. As I thought back upon our visit, I recalled several instances which were evidence of tension and embarrassment. Yet in my mild state of euphoria I had missed them all.

Our insensitivity to the signs of trouble may be more than an assumption that everything is well; we also *want* it to be well. This desire of the pastor to see the smooth and harmonious—or is it a reluctance to see the problems?—may cause him to ignore the signs when he sees them. Instead of following them up he actually flees from them. Another means of escape is to pour on reassurance. "I am sure everything will be all right." "Don't take it too seriously." "It doesn't pay to worry." "We all have our peculiarities." "That's the way life goes." Although these popular clichés have a great deal of truth in them, when they are used by the pastor in response to the allusions his people make to their problems, thy usually end the discussion—but not the problem. And he has given his parishioner little encouragement to come to him for counseling in regard to his problem.

The symptom of a personality problem that stirs up a great

deal of strife is the hypercritical attitude. Critical people in the church often condemn their fellow members in the name of righteousness and religion. When the pastor calls, they tell him how reprehensible his predecessor was. In an indirect way he may take this as an indication that they are on his side. Let him not be taken in; the big guns could just as easily turn on him. He can alienate these people by disagreeing with them; he can get himself dangerously entangled if he allies himself with them.

The *judgmental* attitude is a manifestation of resentment. It is an antisocial compensation for feelings of rejection and failure. If the pastor responds to a critical attitude according to the principles of counseling, he is treating it like the problem that it is. In time this counseling approach may have its effect. The "counselee" may gain a more objective view of things through the counseling process and begin to see that at least some of the problem is in himself. When he does, he will have less need to be critical. If the pastor succeeds in helping him, he will also have reduced a source of friction in his congregational life.

Difficulties in Family Relationships

The deep-seated problems in the human personality often come to the surface as family problems. When the pastor visits in the homes of his people, he is in the center of the problem environment, and the hints of trouble that his people drop are often in regard to family relationships. Chief among these are marriage, children, and in-laws.

Rather than being the panacea for problems that sweethearts envision, marriage can just as easily be the "jump from the frying pan into the fire." It all depends on the people involved. After the honeymoon is over, husband and wife begin to discover that marriage is a more complicated way of life than the single life. When a man and woman join hands to share life, they form a democratic social unit that demands emotional maturity on the part of both. The shortcomings of character that cause problems within the personality also cause problems in marriage. The therapeutic bond of love in marriage is endangered by the self-centered tendencies of the partners. The delicate balance of emotion and the integration of purpose that characterize the consummation of the sexual union are symbolic of the challenging adjustment of the whole of marriage, in which two become one in flesh and spirit in all of life. When this adjustment is not made adequately, an intolerable situation is created within the home—a situation that is responsible for a great deal of drunkenness and promiscuity, myriad mental and physical illnesses, and innumerable instances of suicide and murder. It has been estimated that only ten per cent of all marriages are happy. Even if this estimation is low, the pastor is wise to remind himself as he steps into a house of the possibility that this may be the home that needs his help. When people are having marital difficulty, it is so pressing upon their minds that the alert pastor who calls consistently upon his people will usually have little trouble discerning the signs.

Parenthood is one of the most difficult tasks on earth. Yet most parents "fall into" the job with even less preparation than they had for their marriage. Their problems begin when their child grows out of the cuteness of babyhood, if they do not begin before. Even those who read the latest in child care and psychology become frustrated time and again because their Johnny does not always seem to respond according to the book. Most parents on occasion feel they are failures even before their children arrive at adolescence, but when they take the full brunt of this rebellious age, they may feel absolutely helpless to cope with it.

The personalities of young people bear the imprint of their home. When I counsel with a student with serious problems of personality, I usually find that the source of his trouble is his conflict with his parents. These conflicts are no more pleasant to the parents than to the child, and they can keep a home in an uproar. The parent needs to talk over these conflicts and problems with a counselor. Yet he usually has a tremendous amount of pride in the matter of his parenthood and hates to admit his failure. At the heart of these parental difficulties one will usually find the unsolved personality problems of the parent. When the pastor calls in the home, he may run into one of these conflicts in action. A negative remark by the parent may be the opening which he can follow up in a tactful manner. Once the situation has been disclosed to the pastor, the way is open for him to inquire about it again; because the subject has been brought up before, the parent feels more free to discuss it with him again. In this manner the calling ministry can open to pastoral counseling this area of life that so decidedly influences the future generation.

The mother-in-law, perennial subject for jokes, is more in need of help than of jibes, for an in-law relationship is a difficult adjustment. At the marriage of their son or daughter, parents who have held a governing position over their child must yield their authority and become sages who do not interfere. The new entrant into the family is not always prepared to accept another set of parents, and cannot take their idiosyncrasies for granted as does his mate, who has grown up with them. The situation is conducive to irritation and misunderstanding. In the midst of our strong emphasis upon premarital counseling and of preparing the young couple for this new adjustment to their own and the other's parents, there has been little or no attempt to encourage pre-in-law counseling for the parents. If both families have their own home where they can exercise their freedom, they can better learn to adjust to their new relatives and to their role as an in-law. Put them together in one house, where the irritations have no intermission, and there may be tension and strife.

The proverb that no house is big enough for two families has its exceptions. Yet most people require a certain amount of privacy for relaxation and morale. They like a place they can call their own, where they can be alone and "let their hair down." If the two families in one house are in-laws, the chances for dissatisfaction and friction are even greater, as the rivalries inherent in the in-law relationship are continually stimulated and may develop into growing resentment. This resentment needs an outlet, or it may explode in scenes of temper to cause serious damage. This danger is present also when elderly parents break up their home to move in with their children.

The pastor may be able to release some of this resentment if he manages to call upon such a home, particularly when one of the families is not around. By simply asking in a conversational way how things are going, he may get a response that indicates the presence of dissatisfaction. If he follows this up with a counseling approach, he may not only be the outlet for the resentment that might otherwise cause trouble, but may also assist them better to adapt to their situation, or, if possible, to improve it.

Those Inactive Members

Almost all churches have their roster of inactive members. These people are a burden on the pastor's mind; they dishearten him as they miss the service Sunday after Sunday. He feels he ought to go to them and try to persuade them to be more faithful. Consequently the inactive members usually receive a greater proportion of the pastor's calls than their number would warrant. So far as the relationship between his calling and his counseling is concerned, these numerous calls upon inactive members are a promising investment of his time. Delinquency in church attendance is often either the result of or the prelude to personal problems.

When people have problems, particularly problems that cause them to feel ashamed or bitter, they may stay away from church. Many people have the idea that church is for the good instead of the repentant, for the righteous rather than the convicted sinner. A person who feels guilty over something may find the church atmosphere distressing and uncomfortable because it brings him face to face with God and holiness, and he feels hypocritical and out of place. When an individual has an experience that causes him to become resentful or bitter, his resentment may extend also to the God who permits such things to happen and may lead to a subconscious or even conscious agnosticism. He gives expression to these feelings by staying away from church.

People whose absence from church reveals no pressing problems are opening themselves to problems by their absence. When they get out of the habit of going to church, their spiritual life usually begins to suffer, because there is nothing else in their life to interrupt or to challenge their preoccupation with the tangible and the material. Their sense of values becomes oriented to the things that are temporal and that ultimately leave them unsatisfied, if not disillusioned. In the meantime their motive for morality is weakened and their trend to a self-centered personality is unchallenged. When a person gets away from God, he can easily fall into a pattern of living that leads only to trouble.

Because a good church attendance is considered an indication of his success as a minister, the pastor may lose sight of the connection between absenteeism and trouble, and treat the symptom as though it were the problem. "If I had one area of my ministry that I could do over," said a retired pastor, "I would choose the calling upon inactive members. In my second chance I would not make it my aim to get these people to church once in a while—most people on occasion will yield to pressure from a pastor whom they like—but rather to get them honestly to look into why it is they choose not to attend."

When the Opportunity Presents Itself

The pastor who calls upon his people in a manner sympathetic to counseling will find opportunities for counseling in his calling. He must be prepared to respond to these when they come. During the conversation of the call or perhaps at its close, the parishioner may indicate to the pastor that there are a few things she would like to talk to him about sometime. She is giving him the hint, and it is up to him not to ignore it but to respond to it. In a way that is devoid of coercion he may indicate his willingness to talk with her and ask when it would be convenient for her. She in turn will usually be concerned also about his convenience, and the result may be an appointment satisfactory to both.

Instead of alluding to the fact that she would like to talk to him, the parishioner may say things during the call that an alert pastor will perceive as hints to the presence of a problem. When he follows up these hints, the problem itself may suddenly come out in the open. The pastor is now faced with a decision. Should he proceed to counsel with the person? Or should he suggest a counseling appointment? Like any other decision this one also has its pros and cons. Will there be enough time to discuss the problem at the present? Does the pastor have an engagement shortly that he must keep? Since they are in the parishioner's home, will they be interrupted by the entry of other members of the family at an inconvenient time? Since the discussion of a personal problem often leads to a show of emotion and even tears, would an interruption be embarrassing to all concerned?

On the other hand, should he not strike when the iron is hot? Is there not a danger that a postponement may cause a person to change her mind about discussing her problem? A person's situation or mood may have changed by the time of the appointment so that she no longer feels the desire to discuss her problem. Of course, people can sometimes be brought around again by conversation to their problem. These are the considerations that the pastor must face in making his decision, which, of necessity, may differ in accordance with situation. On the whole, I would lean toward going as far with the counseling as time allowed when the opportunity presented itself.

The visitation-evangelism program that is being stressed in contemporary congregational life is closely related to the counseling program in the approach of the caller upon the un-churched. As an example, a recent text in evangelism suggests that the caller not try to answer the flimsy excuses that people often give for not attending church but rather that he restate the excuse and get the individual to elaborate on it so that he will see for himself that it is not his real reason. In this manner every call upon the unchurched becomes a potential counseling situation. Home missionaries are often hindered in converting this potential into an actuality by the large number of calls per month that they are required to make by their denominational mission board. This means that the caller may lose sight of the deeper possibilities of each call in his concentration on fulfilling his quota. This also means that each call has to be limited in time to the point where counseling clues may not as yet ma-terialize.

Personal work in the office of the ministry is not confined to counseling and calling. In the entire field of church adminis-tration the pastor works with people. These contacts that he has with people in his administrative work are also of vital sig-nificance to his counseling ministry.

CHAPTER EIGHT

Administrative Work and Counseling

THE CHRISTIAN CHURCH TRACES ITS HISTORY TO THE DAY OF
Pentecost, when through the inspired witness of the apostles
three thousand people asked for baptism. Shortly after this the
number of members is listed by the book of Acts as five thousand.
Because of the early emphasis on Christianity as a way of life
the church grew not only in numbers but also in the exercise
of a fellowship which extended even to the sharing of material
possessions through the common treasury. The twelve apostles
who were trained by Christ were the organized leadership of
the church. In the press of ever-increasing duties they began
to hear murmurs against their manner of administering the
common treasury. Realizing that the trouble lay in the human
limitations of having too much to do, they requested the congregation to select seven laymen to take care of this distribution
of funds. When these men, who were called deacons, were
chosen, the church vestry was born, and the administration of
the church began to keep pace with the growth in membership
and in opportunities.

After nineteen hundred years of sporadic development the
church is the most highly organized in its history. Its administration has developed to the extent that even the modest congregation often has the organizational structure of a modern business
enterprise. Heading up this complex administrative skeleton—

in the role of the executive secretary—is the pastor. Most theological students think of the ministry in terms of preaching and pastoral care, and have little comprehension of or sympathy for the executive function of the office. Seminary curricula are also usually lacking in courses that prepare the student for this ministry of administration. As a result the young pastor often steps into the parish ministry neither expectant nor trained to handle this difficult challenge in organization. His role as an administrator, however, so permeates the congregational life that it has a direct bearing upon his other activities and in particular upon his counseling ministry.

In the organization program of the congregation the pastor is dealing with people in a corporation setting. His role differs greatly from that of the business executive, however, since the pastor's is an organization of volunteers. Beside being unable to fire the incompetent and hire the capable, he must curry the good will of both. In spite of this restriction he must see that the program of the church not only carries on but also expands.

The projects of the parish organization, therefore, are close to the pastor's heart. He wants them to succeed because he believes they are of value to the kingdom of God and also because in their success he too succeeds. Whatever or whoever threatens the success of these projects is also threatening the pastor's ambitions. It is a real challenge to any pastor to maintain a benevolent objectivity in dealing with problems that seem to be a menace to his own plans. Yet it is in meeting this challenge that he not only prevents his role as an administrator from interfering with his counseling ministry but also uses it in support of this ministry. And his administrative program also will come through much better in the end because of this approach.

Frustrations in Administration

Those who cause the difficulties in the organized work of the church are often people with problems and the very ones

91

who need counseling. The presence of reactionaries on the church vestry is a thorn in many a pastor's side. These are the men who may pride themselves on being sensible and practical but who actually are negative characters and obstacles to progress. I know of one vestryman who responds to every constructive proposal by saying, "Now do not misunderstand me; I am not saying how I feel about this thing. But just to get the ball rolling, I move that we don't do it." A defensive attitude toward progress is a problem of personality and is often caused by the abhorrence of parting with one's money or by the fear that expansion in the program would reduce one's importance.

The neurotic woman in the ladies' society can stir up plenty of trouble. Hypercritical in her attitude and vicious with her tongue, she tangles with the other ladies in the work of the group. By putting two and two together and getting five, she comes up with gossip disruptive to the harmony of the entire congregation. Usually she is an unhappy person. Feeling frustrated, she takes her resentment out on others. She needs help.

The young people's society can be the pastor's joy or the pastor's trial. The rapid turnover in membership due to the narrow age bracket of this group means a fluctuating organization. It is frustrating to see your young leaders go off to college and leave the youth group with no replacements. As one pastor put it, "A couple of years ago I had a swell bunch of kids in my youth group, but these that I have in there now! Honestly— sometimes I'd just like to bop their heads together!" Evidently he has an immature group with few, if any, capable of assuming responsibility or exercising leadership.

The work of the congregation is dependent upon volunteer service. Unfortunately, the willing are not always the able. Those who accept an assignment do not always complete it. Those on a committee do not always come to the meetings. Most churches have had their deacons who did not serve, their teachers who failed to show up on Sunday morning, and their calling committees who always intended but never got around to making their calls. In the meantime the pastor is counting on these people. He finds out only too often that the things he thought were taken care of are really the things that did not get done. If he tries to prevent this from happening by doing things himself, he is depriving his people of learning to assume responsibility and taking upon himself more than he can possibly do. If he tries to prevent it by continuously checking up on his workers, he may develop a reputation of being a Simon Legree. In this case his workers may begin to feel sheepish in his presence and take advantage of opportunities to avoid him. The loss of rapport in this manner is unfortunate, because it is often problems in personality that cause individuals to be negligent in their duties.

Beside those who fail to respond to their duties, there are also those who respond in a negative way. Either they do not come to the meetings or they come and say nothing, but in either case they say plenty in criticism afterward. Others accept an assignment and begin their work, but something goes wrong, and they get their feelings hurt. In protest they may threaten to quit their task and even the church, or they may withdraw in silence to nurse their grievance.

As if the peculiarities of people were not enough, the pastor is often harassed also by physical limitations to his program. The facilities of the building may be inadequate for a progressive Sunday school or for an attractive youth program. And of course the church treasury is usually even more inadequate and a continual irritant to the execution of his ideas.

Each person with whom the pastor deals in his administrative capacity is a potential counselee. The most unlikely character ever to enter the pastor's office may be the one whom the changes of the future will bring into a counseling relationship. The pastor therefore must keep the door open for such opportunities even in the face of frustrating people and exasperating circumstances. For the sake of his personal ministry he must have patience when others lose it; he must believe in people when others consider them hopeless; he must understand those whom others judge according to their prejudices. By so doing he will be in a position to help these people when the opportunity presents itself. When he helps them with their personal problems, he is ministering also to the problem role they play in the administrative work of the church.

The Counseling Approach in Administration

As divergent as the pastoral activities of administration and counseling appear, they are actually quite closely related. The pastor's attitude in the pursuit of either is likely to influence his approach in the other. If his past failure as a counselor is charged to his dogmatic attitude, this same spirit is ruinous in his administrative work. In former days the prestige of the role of the pastor in many churches discouraged lay leadership. His personage carried with it an authority that was almost synonymous with the administration of the congregation. (His financial limitations, however, were even more restrictive than they are today.) He was often the only man with higher education in the congregation. People respected him—but at times to the point of being afraid of him. This is the way one pastor described how he felt toward his own pastor as a child: "Pastor Adams had a short-cropped beard. When he would get mad, that beard would go up and down. We kids were scared to death of him. When he was around, we really behaved ourselves. But as far as going to him with our problems—we couldn't have stood it." This type of pastoral bearing was neither conducive to a voluntary counseling program nor to a congregation bustling with the creative activity of its laymen.

The emergence of the principles of counseling with their re-emphasis on the priesthood of the believer has been a counter-active influence to this paternalistic spirit. The pastor who follows these principles in his relationship to his people in the counseling room will in all probability be influenced by these principles in his dealings with his people around the table of administration. Even as these principles in their adaptation to the calling ministry form a pattern for a good conversationalist, so in their adaptation to organizational work they form a sort of administrative philosophy.

In meetings with his workers or in speaking individually to them he encourages them to express their opinions. He tries to see their point in controversial issues. He respects their suggestions in the same manner as he would expect them to respect his. He encourages them to experiment with their creative ideas. As a leader he has ideas of his own and keeps before his people, through enthusiasm and logical clarity, the constructive program upon which they are working or should be working. In this manner he is inspiring them to grow and to develop their potential for leadership in the church. This is the spirit described in the verse of scripture often used in the ordination service: "Neither as being lords over God's heritage, but being ensamples to the flock" (I Pet. 5:3).

Dangers to Counseling

Yesterday's patriarchal lord has been superseded by today's jolly despot. This is the pastor who has become infatuated with his role as a leader. In gatherings of his people he is the social promoter who abounds in personality as he tries to keep everybody happy. He associates being a leader with being loud. He sings loudly, prays loudly, laughs loudly, talks loudly, whether he needs to or not. Although his people may be impressed by these qualities, those with personality problems will be discouraged from coming to him because of them. Although they may envy him these qualities, they feel miles apart from him in their difficulties. This gap makes it hard for them to see how he could understand them, and also makes them feel even more inferior in his presence.

Actually he dominates more than he leads. His motivation seems to stem from a compulsion to hold to the center of everybody's attention. In the counseling situation he must give the center to the counselee. Not only is it difficult for him to make this radical transition, but his traditional bearing gives the counselee no indication that he will even try. So he is reluctant to come to him.

The description of this counseling approach to administration is essentially the description of the democratic process—a conclusion to which we could have logically arrived, since the principles of counseling and the fundamentals of democracy have a common doctrinal origin in the priesthood of the believer. It is in the face of this democratic procedure that the pastor meets a strong challenge to his integrity, and his reaction to this challenge greatly affects his counseling ministry, since there is a direct correlation between the character of the pastor and his value as a counselor.

Democracy breaks down when people become afraid of it. The pastor may fear it when it poses as a threat to his plans. In taking precautions against this danger he may abuse the democratic procedure rather than use it. To insure the adoption of his ideas he may knowingly give the congregation inadequate or even biased information. He may resort to intimidation by veiled threats or subtle ridicule, and thereby succumb to the infamous practice of "railroading." Because he has retained the form of democracy but has violated its spirit, his actions are basically dishonest.

Though he transcend the temptation to sabotage the democratic procedure, the administrative dangers to his character continue in the atmosphere of democratic decision. When men are free to speak their minds, they often speak *too* freely as emotions rise and egos are stimulated. The pastor also is a man of pride and passion, and almost before he realizes it, he may be engaging in verbal combat at a level which can only lower him in the estimation of his people. They are sensitive to anything in administrative conversation which seems to be in contrast to what he himself has told them is the Christian way. These emotional outbursts may occur simply because he is human. If there are no further irritations, they can be lived down and often rather quickly. People know that the pastor needs an outlet for his emotions also and that his main trouble was in his unfortunate selection of the time and place. Time spent before a meeting contemplating the dangers he may face is often the mental preparation needed to resist the tempter at the critical moment.

The pastor's prestige is a tremendous power in parish policy, and therefore he has a serious moral responsibility in his use of it. If his leadership is strong, the democratic procedure is automatically weakened on issues where he has taken a stand. His personality may overwhelm the opposition. Many a layman has felt defeated not by the workings of democracy or the appeal to reason but by the disadvantage of the pastor's prestige. Yet the pastor has to reckon with the possibility that his leadership may not be strong and that even if it is, he may still face defeat when he submits his plans to a written ballot. And sometimes it happens. Since his plans were very important to him, he meets an even greater test of character.

Any immaturity in his personality may come out at this time in terms of temper remarks or childish reprisals. He may also become engulfed in gloom and lose his incentive for continued service. Subconsciously, at least, the layman feels let down by this all-too-human reaction to defeat, and as a result is more repelled than attracted to his pastor's counseling ministry. Also the pastor seems to be so weighed down by his own problems that the layman would feel guilty in coming to him with more problems. Yet what counseling he is able to conduct during this period will help him forget his own troubles. When the counselee and his problem become the focal point of attention, he actually loses himself in the lives of others. The concentration that is demanded of him as a listener comes almost naturally as he assumes a counselor role and is a welcome relief from his own depressing thoughts.

On the other hand, if he can take the defeat in the spirit of one who does not lean on his own understanding but acknowledges God in all his ways, his example may ultimately accomplish more than his proposed plans. People will not feel sorry for him after his defeat, and this in itself prevents a barrier to his counseling ministry. Being able to feel comfortable in the presence of one who has experienced defeat strengthens our confidence in his ability to understand and to help.

The Needs of the Pastor-Administrator

Since the administrative work of the pastor affects his counseling program, his challenge is to make this influence favorable. To do this he needs to cultivate certain qualities of the spirit: a Christian sense of values, a workable faith in God, and an objective approach to problems.

A Christian sense of values. "Seek ye first the kingdom of God, and his righteousness; and all these things shall be added unto you." (Matt. 6:33.) With these words Jesus gave to his church its scale of values. When the pastor's ego gets involved in his administrative work, other motives than the search for the Kingdom are at hand; his religion has become contaminated. How has this happened? Another administrator, James, in the Letter generally ascribed to him, has an answer: "Pure religion and undefiled before God and the Father is this, To visit the fatherless and widows in their affliction, and to keep himself unspotted from the world" (1:27). The closer we come to putting the Kingdom first, the more importance we place upon the individual and his needs. The antagonist to this Christian sense of values is the world about us. Although it has a veneer of Christianity, ours is a success-maddened society that puts a terrific competitive pressure on its citizens to climb to the top in positions of prestige.

In a special way the pastor is called of God to visit the fatherless and the widows in their affliction—those who are in need of comfort and counsel. In a very real sense he is also in danger of being spotted by the success philosophy of the world. The

98

office of the ministry has not escaped the world's system of evaluation. In this environment he may feel constrained to push himself to success by advancing in the ranks. He wants to take the applauded path to the big church with its big audience, big budget, big membership, big prestige, and, since it seems to go with it, its big salary. Inwardly it is the struggle between love and pride for dominance in his motivation. If pride should win, the victories of his administration may be gained at a sacrifice to the kingdom of God.

Pride is an insidious thing; it creeps up on a person without his knowing it. The best defense against it is to keep it before you—not behind you. The pastor who realizes he has pride and that it is a continual threat to his ministry is the pastor most likely to keep pride from dominating him. Since pride stands in direct opposition to a Christian sense of values, the best offense against it is to saturate the mind with the meaning of pure religion. This means that in the midst of the hectic and never-ending day of pastoral administration, the pastor will take time out to reorient his mind to the value scale of the Kingdom.

A workable faith in God. In his book *My Six Convicts,* the psychologist Donald Powell Wilson gives a very appealing description of the Roman Catholic chaplain of Fort Leavenworth Penitentiary as a pastoral counselor. Among other things Father Dowd had a "respectful, absorbed way of listening that made one feel he was the kind of man God would be smart to talk to when he had anything special to say. He could be disappointed without being discouraged and in a penitentiary this was essential equipment." This same equipment is essential also in the parish ministry. It is the result of a workable faith in God. Sometimes the hardest place for the pastor to practice the trust he preaches is in the ups and downs of his own parish program.

From the experience of the apostle Paul, who had "the care of all the churches" upon him daily, comes a formula for the

99

practice of faith (Phil. 4:6-7). Broken up into its four directives, it can be adapted to the pastor-administrator as follows:

1. "Be careful [full of care] for nothing"—not even the building program.

2. "But in every thing by prayer and supplication . . . let your requests be made known unto God"—even about the deacon who has taken a dislike to you.

3. "With thanksgiving"—in remembrance of his past deliverances.

4. "And the peace of God, which passeth all understanding, shall keep your hearts and minds through Christ Jesus." Everything is under control. God will see it through.

The activity of faith makes inactive the negative feelings of fear, resentment, and discouragement that cause us conflict, corrupt our motives, and ruin our example. One cannot judge the present while it is still the present. Today is only a fragment which is uninterpretable until it fits into the story that is told. "All things *work together* for good to them that love God, to them who are the called according to his purpose." (Rom. 8:28.) Every defeat is ultimately a victory. A life of faith is a thrilling adventure; anything can happen, because all things are possible. The pastor can transcend the frustrations of the moment because he has within him "the evidence of things not seen."

An objective approach to problems. When we think back to the occasions which at the time were sources of irritation, they seem to be more humorous than irritating. When we look back, we are inclined to see the situation more objectively. Actually irritating situations are humorous. If we could only view them more objectively *when they occur,* we would see the humor and escape the irritation. This means that we may have to laugh at ourselves also. A sense of humor is an invaluable aid to pastoral administration. It is also a mark of a mature person.

Maturity is not something we have attained but something toward which we are growing. While we are still in the process of "becoming," we will profit from the advice of the presiding

100

elder of the convention of the church in Jerusalem, which was called to settle the explosive question of circumcision. "Wherefore, my beloved brethren, let every man be swift to hear, slow to speak, slow to wrath: for the wrath of man worketh not the righteousness of God." (James 1:19-20.) It almost sounds as though James had learned this the hard way.

The favorable contacts that the pastor has with his people in the course of his administrative work are needed for the development of his counseling program. I know of one pastor who is so hasty in his criticism and so petulant in his demands that his people are reluctant to work with him. I know of another who would rather do the work himself than use his laymen, because, as he says, they do such a poor job at things that he ends up doing it himself anyway. In developing these qualities of the spirit that we have discussed, the pastor will find release from this perfectionist obsession. He will be free to adapt himself to an imperfect world and to accept the limitations of his people and of himself. He will enjoy working with his people, and they will enjoy working with him.

In the close quarter of administrative detail people get to know their pastor as in no other way. Sooner or later they will see the real man. In so doing they are able to perceive the quality that draws them most of all to his counseling ministry; they are in a position to perceive his sincerity. This will show through even though he may blunder here and there. In fact, it would take a great many blunders to undermine the people's respect for a pastor they know is trying to give them his best.

CHAPTER NINE

Developing the Spiritual Life

THE CHURCH IS THE INSTITUTION THAT IS DIVINELY COMMIS-
sioned to help people to know God. It can learn much from
the secular world that will help in carrying out this function. But
if the church fails in the area of its own specialty, regardless of
how well it can simulate the secular skills, it has failed those
who have come to it for help. When people come to the church,
they are searching for answers to the questionings of their spiritual nature—they want to know about God, about death, about
purpose, about truth. The pastor as the representative of the
church represents this speciality. He may be an excellent psychologist, but if he is not able to dispense the wisdom of his
religious heritage, he is not what people come to him for. He
is a counselor—not a pastoral counselor.

The Role of Leader to Learner

While pastoral counseling most certainly includes the knowledge of psychiatric principles, it also goes beyond these principles. Beside the counselor-counselee relationship there is the
leader-learner relationship, which in the historical terminology
of religion is that of master to disciple. It is the master who
holds the key to the success of this relationship, since it is having
something to give that precipitates the gathering of those who
would receive. The pastor's role as leader in this religious relationship depends upon the development of his own spiritual life.
Ironically the ministry is one of the easiest places to neglect this

development. The schedule of activities of the contemporary pastor is increasing to the point of becoming impossible. Something has to give—and too often it is those activities for which there is no immediate accounting. Among them is the cultivation of his own inner growth.

The pastor is aware of this neglect, but the impossible demands upon his time offer what appears to be an impenetrable defense. Ultimately this rationalization is exposed for what it is—a choice of values incommensurate with the ideology of his calling. Before him is the example of his own Master. In our preoccupation over our dizzy pace we often forget that two thousand years ago a Man accomplished more in three years than any dozen moderns put together accomplish in a lifetime. In the midst of a harried schedule of continuous preaching, teaching, counseling, administering, and traveling, Jesus was untouched by the occupational hazards of tension and fatigue. The reason is obvious throughout the pages of the Gospels. The Lord always saw to it that he had time for prayer. Sometimes it meant staying up all night, at other times, climbing a mountain or crossing the lake, and on occasion, searching for retreat beyond the borders of Palestine. It was these withdrawals for communion with his Father that gave him the vitality to succeed in his mission. His disciplined life does not depend upon his being divine, but upon his being human in the way God intended human beings to be.

Luther understood the value of Jesus' way. His approach to busyness is counter to the current trend. "I am so busy now," he said, "that if I did not spend two or three hours each day in prayer, I could not get through the day."

The Consequences of Neglect

The pastor who neglects his spiritual development soon loses his message. When this happens, there begins a subtle substitution of the intellectual for the religious. His theology becomes his religion rather than the intellectual expression of his religion. His is a knowledge about, rather than a knowing. Although this is an inward condition, it is externally perceptible to the sensitive who need help. "I know whom I believe in and am persuaded—," is tremendously different from, "I know about whom we believe in, for we have been told—." The result so far as his counseling is concerned is that he begins to pass out simple advice for complicated problems. He fails to see the intricate emotional conflicts behind these problems because he has ceased to recognize his own emotional needs. This kind of therapy may not be of much help to people. As a result he may become impatient with the sufferers. He may reach the conclusion that the more irritating are just plain self-centered. Because he is unable to see the emotional causes for self-centeredness, he acts as though the counselee is more in need of judgment than of understanding. His attitude is unacceptive and blocks the relationship that is needed to help the counselee to overcome.

The problem goes back to the fact that the pastor who has not faced his own problems cannot have the understanding that is needed to help others. Not only his busy schedule but also, as we have noted, the pressure on his character is an obstacle to facing his inner needs. The pastor may feel he cannot let down like others or he would ruin his role in his people's minds. Consequently he may tend to build his faith on sheer determination rather than on any victorious encounter with his spiritual enemies. Because so many lean on him as their support for religion, he feels the weight of his responsibility so greatly that he may bypass the dark night of the soul for fear that all he has given to others might collapse if he faced it. Since he feels he cannot afford to have slips in faith like others, he is prevented from being honest with himself when he has the common conflicts within. These conflicts can become chastening experiences that create a stronger faith when they are frankly recognized instead of ignored.

The Pastor's Need for a Counselor

A minister has to "get things off his chest" even as do others. He too may need a counselor. The pastor's wife often serves in this capacity. He can confide in her his frustrations and disappointments, as well as his hopes and plans. The wise layman within the congregation is another human outlet for the pastor. Such a person often has the advantage of past experience with the congregation and can be a real help to the pastor as an understanding friend and adviser.

There are, however, limitations in the counseling roles of both the pastor's wife and the layman within the congregation. The wife may not be objective enough to hear about the deacon who is abusing her husband. Her sympathetic disturbance may cause the pastor to become even more disturbed. As irritated as he may become at an obdurate vestryman, he had better not complain about him to the sympathetic vestryman. This is the sort of familiarity with one's laymen that can lead to contempt. It is a good rule not to talk about one member to another except honestly to praise him.

What is needed in these instances is the pastor's pastor—the district president, bishop, or whoever he may be. It is unfortunate that administrative details often hinder these officials of the church from performing this service to the pastors under their guidance. Considering the tensions that abound in the work of the ministry, I wonder whether there is any task more important for these overseers than to be available as the pastor's pastor. There may also be among the local ministers a pastor who, though serving a congregation of his own, is by virtue of his person the one to whom other pastors take their problems. In any case, the pastor should not hesitate to seek out his "father confessor" among the clergy when he feels the need to talk over his problems with a fellow human being.

If the pastor is especially disturbed, he may need the help of a professional psychotherapist—psychiatrist or clinical psychologist. I have known pastors who have used this resource, and in addition to receiving help in their own emotional problems, they have found it an experience of tremendous value for their counseling ministry.

Counseling with God

The way to become a good counselor is to be a counselee. In addition to human counseling the pastor needs divine counseling. In a very real way God can be the pastor's Counselor. It is this counseling relationship with God that develops the pastor's spiritual life. The benefits of the pastoral-counseling relationship are indicative of the benefits from a counselee relationship with God. Those who are more or less blocked in their relationship to God find in pastoral counseling a means for initiating or resuming this relationship. The values received from pastoral counseling lead to the fullness of these values in the divine counseling. The pastor also may become blocked in his counseling relationship with God and need the help of a fellow counselor. The purpose, however, is to restore his counseling relationship with God, and not to dispense with it. God can work through a competent psychotherapist to remove the emotional hindrances that prevent prayer from being a therapeutic experience.

The counselor needs this counselee relationship to God simply because he is a counselor. Beside whatever personal problems he may have, he has the care of his counselees. These people can worry him. There may be those who are discouraged because they do not feel they are making any progress. Some show improvement only to fall back again. Others fail to return in their follow-up interviews. The pastor wonders how much he is responsible for these things. Perhaps some of his cases are beyond his ability to help. Then there is that prize worry over the counselee who gives indications of being suicidal. He would not want anything like this on his conscience.

Although he may determine that he is not going to allow these things to bother him, his inner anxiety continues to operate. In the morning when he should be working creatively on his sermon, his mind keeps wandering to the interview he must keep that afternoon with a difficult counselee. At dinner time his family finds him present only in body, as he is mentally preoccupied with his counseling activity of the previous hour. At night his rest is reduced by the anxiety in his subconscious mind that erupts in disturbing dreams and in repeated awakenings. More than one pastor owes his nervous exhaustion or emotional breakdown to his worry over his counselees.

The pastor owes it to himself, his family, and his counselees to take his burden as a counselor to the higher Counselor. This pouring out of our negative feelings in a counseling relationship with God is what Fritz Künkel calls "confessional meditation." [1] It is the combination of the old practice of meditation and prayer with the new practice of depth psychology.

An individual's negative feelings must have an outlet, or they will remain within him to obstruct his growth. The ideal outlet, according to Künkel, is through a counseling relationship with God. Here they are not only released but also resolved. If we would let go with our feelings in God's presence as did the psalmists of the Old Testament, he says, we would not only spend their intensity but would also gain the insights needed for an objective evaluation of our problems for our own maturity. The awareness of the presence of God acts as a magnet drawing us to the original of which we were meant to be the image.

In the manner of "confessional meditation" the pastor can release his buildup of anxiety in the presence of his God, so that he can enforce the mental discipline that he desires. The crucial times of the day are the morning when one prepares

---

[1] *In Search of Maturity* (New York: Chas. Scribner's Sons, 1943), pp. 262 ff.

to face a new day; at the heat of the day, when the wear and tear are at their peak; and at the close of the day, when one prepares emotionally for rest. The psalmist reserves these crucial times for moments of private devotion.

> Evening and morning and at noon
> I utter my complaint and moan,
> and he will hear my voice.
> (Ps. 55:17, R.S.V.)

The devotional life of the prophet Daniel also is characterized by this tripartite division. "He went to his house where he had windows in his upper chamber open toward Jerusalem; and he got down upon his knees three times a day and prayed and gave thanks before his God, as he had done previously." (Dan. 6:10, R.S.V.) This devotional pattern is strategically geared to the needs of the personality, and works in particularly well with the ministerial schedule. The midday period would perhaps be placed between his afternoon activities and his evening meal. Like Peter, he may retire to his "roof" for prayer while dinner is being prepared below. In this manner he encourages himself to commit the unsettled issues of the day to God, so that he may be able to integrate himself into the family program which follows. Periods devoted to the cultivation of relaxation through prayer make possible a faith in God that allows one mentally to put aside problem areas in which he is not at the moment engaged.

A regulated devotional pattern also enables the pastor consistently to bear his counselee's problems to God. It is to any counselee's advantage to have his pastor making intercessory prayer on his behalf. The relationship of the shepherd to his flock is structured of God as an important channel in the medium of prayer. The value of pastoral intercession in no way mitigates the priesthood of the believer; it is rather in addition to the priesthood role. The pastor is one who shares in the responsibility for those who are committed unto his care. God has chosen to work through prayer and through the office of the ministry. Pastoral intercession is the pastor's homework in pastoral counseling.

These conferences with God prepare the pastor for greater efficiency as an instrument of God. They enlarge the vista of his faith by their revelation to his experience of the bigness of God. God is ever conscious of us. It is as we become conscious of him that contact is made. This focus on God is the opening of faith that channels the grace of God to the soul. The pastor's devotional life is the means of making his mind receptive to divine direction. It brings his pastoral counseling directly under the guidance of God. This fact alone means help for the counselee's problem; the pastor's realization of it means a relaxing of his tension. The result is an efficient operation of the divine-human partnership within the framework of the church.

Experience in Sanctification

The pastor's devotional life takes him beyond the first principles of his faith into the vast expanse of sanctification. The writer of the Letter to the Hebrews saw the danger of a blockage between the justification and sanctification processes of spiritual experience in the lives of Christians and appealed to his readers to transcend it.

Therefore let us leave the elementary doctrines of Christ and go on to maturity, not laying again a foundation of repentance from dead works and of faith toward God, with instruction about ablutions, the laying on of hands, the resurrection of the dead, and eternal judgment. And this we will do if God permits. (Heb. 6:1-3, R.S.V.)

Through his devotional life he develops from a *babe in Christ* to a *spiritual man*. No longer needing to be *fed with milk,* he feasts on *solid food.* He is not an *ordinary man.* (I Cor. 3:1-3,

109

R.S.V.) It is through personal experience alone that one knows the way of Christ so that he can impart it to others. The crises that lead to reliance upon God; the surrender to God that brings him within; the experience of his love that slows our resistance to his will; the identification with Christ that triumphs over the self-center—all are stages in the aged and trodden path of victory over the enemies within. One does not learn them as he would learn a formula; rather, he follows one who has gone this way himself.

Jesus said that the purpose of his coming was that we might have life and have it more abundantly. Through his life, death, and resurrection he completed the atonement that brings God to man to make this life possible. The purpose of forgiveness is to restore the fellowship with God that was broken by sin. The extent to which we follow through in this purpose reveals the degree of abundance that we experience. The character of this abundance is described as the fruit of the Spirit. These are the constructive forces of personality that drive out the destructive—love for resentment, faith for anxiety, peace for guilt, joy for despair. "The fruit of the Spirit is love, joy, peace, patience, kindness, goodness, faithfulness, gentleness, self-control; against such there is no law." (Gal. 5:22-23, R.S.V.)

These are the qualities of the *Christ* personality, and they come to us only through fellowshipping with his Spirit. The devotional life holds the key to our growing in every way "unto the measure of the stature of the fulness of Christ." The pastor can scarcely have experienced all the problems with which he will have to deal. Nor is this absolutely necessary. He would not, for example, have had to be a drunkard in order to develop rapport with an alcoholic. Those in Alcoholics Anonymous have known alcoholism by personal experience and have triumphed over it. For this reason they are in a strategic position to redeem the alcoholic, and the wise pastor will utilize the help of this group in his dealings with alcoholics. The alcoholic's basic problem is not the alcoholic hallucination but the need for escape, and this is not confined to alcoholics. The pastor too has experienced it, though he may not have resorted to the particular escape of alcohol. The fruit of the Spirit is developed against the opposition of the destructive emotions. The pastor who has fought the battle with his own reluctance to stand up to the unpleasant realities of his life, may be of help to the alcoholic or to others who feel inadequate and defeated before the demands of life. This is the pastor who shows by his ability to understand that he knows the inner life.

A man's walk with God is perceptible, and people are drawn to his spirituality as by a magnet. The man of God has ever been an anchor in the storm, a rock in the midst of sand, a tower of strength for those who know they are weak. Down through the centuries such men have been the successful counselors. They knew nothing about counseling as a science, but intuitively they followed its principles. The experience of struggle and triumph within their own souls was their teacher. Yet their learning was accompanied by a spirit for which no principles can substitute. They are men who have been with Jesus, and this fact cannot be hidden. As people asked their Master—"Lord, teach us to pray"—so they ask these ministers of his—"Pastor, teach me to have faith."

Knowledge of the Devotional Life

If pastoral counseling leads to counseling with God, guidance in the devotional life is indispensable to pastoral counseling. The pastor's own experience with the devotional life is his source material for this guidance. People are often blocked in the area of personal devotions. Usually they are eager for any help the pastor can give to improve their efficiency in this endeavor, which they realize is fundamental to their spiritual development. These people frequently are hindered in their approach to God by their own feelings of unworthiness before him. Through the counseling process these feelings of guilt can be exposed and resolved so that an attitude of acceptance before God may develop. These same people may also lack in knowledge of the mechanics of personal devotions, and feel helpless before any directive to read the Bible or pray. They would not know how to begin. They may read suggested devotional booklets, but these are often merely brief sermonettes. Simply reading through a devotional program may not produce the experience of communion with God.

It is this experience of communion that the pastor with a productive devotional life can help his counselees achieve. He has learned how to use the Scriptures to find help in his own problems. He knows the art of listening to God, which is so necessary a part of the conversation of prayer. He has discovered how to expose his mind to the influence of the divine Mind through concentration upon the spirit and expression of the Word. Because of this he can present his counselees with a devotional pattern and the spiritual resources that will enable them to experience this same spiritual development. Because he is aware of the psychological differences within people, he will present his suggestions in line with the individual qualities of the counselee. Since this fellowshipping with the Spirit leads to those spiritual qualities that bring harmony to the soul, the devotional program of the counselee is a vital supplement to the pastoral-counseling process.

Naturally we pastors feel inadequate before such a task. We know in our own hearts the shortcomings in our spiritual life and often feel the need for this help ourself. Even this is not necessarily a drawback. The experience of dry periods in the devotional life is not abnormal. Our learning to deal with this sort of mood can be passed on. We are the pastors. Others are dependent upon us for this spiritual leadership. Our course is outlined for us by the Master himself. He had given his disciples powers to use in helping people. They, however, had to have the faith to use them. While he was on the mountain with his chosen three, the nine below were presented with the problem of the demon-possessed lad. They tried to help—but they failed. Disturbed and puzzled, they asked the Master why. Because you lacked in faith, he told them. How could they get this faith? "This kind cannot be driven out by anything but prayer" (R.S.V.). The answer is plain—the rest depends upon the determination of the pastor.

CHAPTER TEN

Scholarship in the Field

ESSENTIALLY THE MINISTER IS A STUDENT. BEFORE HE CAN function in the office, he must satisfy scholarship requirements, which usually are quite lengthy. Theological seminaries are, theoretically at least, graduate schools. The pastor is the man of the Book—and of books. Like any teacher, he must also be a learner. It is not without reason that his office is referred to as the study.

His counseling also requires that he be always the student. Practical experience alone will not satisfy this need—any more than book learning alone equips a man for any position. Both are needed, for each stimulates the productivity of the other. Without study the counselor would become ingrown. His ability to interpret what is happening so that he can make the proper response depends upon his knowledge of the field. When this knowledge is not stimulated by other minds, it tends to fade in the fine points. If we do not continue to add to what we have, we begin to lose even that which we do have. The pastor who ceases to be a student will sooner or later impoverish himself and his people. What he has keeps getting thinner and thinner, but he rarely realizes this while it is happening. When one goes at the pace of the contemporary minister, it is almost impossible for him to notice any change that is gradual. He realizes the situation only after it has happened. His mind is so concentrated on the events of the external world that internal pursuits such as evaluation are postponed indefinitely.

The Need for Study

The study of human nature is not an objective science. Men cannot study themselves without seeing themselves through their own eyes. Any distortion of his ego shows itself in the scientist's interpretation of the human psyche. When he continually relies on his own evaluative processes, he develops a sense of sufficiency that in itself is blinding. When this happens to the counselor, he gets in a rut and misses the clues that often make the difference between helping people to solve their problems and giving them a little relief. Without outside stimulation his vision becomes increasingly narrow. If he balances his own observations and theories with a study of the insights and conclusions of others, he is often surprised at the areas he has overlooked. His own deductions may then appear superficial to him. He becomes perturbed as he realizes that he has learned some of these subtleties in previous days, but evidently they have become dulled in his mind when he has failed to keep them alive by the discipline of review.

As an example, I was impressed by the discovery that over half of those who had come to me for counseling did not present their real problem when they came. I accounted for this in terms of the natural hesitance of people to talk about issues in their lives that are charged with negative emotions, and particularly shame. It was through my reading on the subject that I realized that people may not know what their real problem is when they first come—that it is only through the counseling process that the excavation takes place that brings it to light. I knew of this "burial process" before. Yet it took this review with the background of further experience to bring it to the point of application.

This does not mean that the pastor must concentrate his scholarship in the field of pastoral counseling. Even as the counseling ministry is related to the other areas of the ministry, so also the literature in these other fields is related to counseling.

The study of theology deals with the needs of the human personality even as does psychology, and theology's answers to these needs are intimately related to the counseling process. On the other hand, the study of psychology furnishes the minister with a concept of the inner dynamics of personality that assist him in applying his theological resources. Scholarship in the related field of the social sciences is producing helpful data on marriage and the family, church and community, that broadens the vision of the counselor.

Since the counseling process easily matures into an educational relationship, the study of religious education has its carry-over for the counselor. The science of leadership development provides insight into maturity and acceptance of responsibility that coincides with the goal of the counseling process. Literature on the spiritual life and its disciplines is an indirect preparation for the distinctly pastoral end of pastoral counseling. By the same token, works in pastoral psychology and counseling assist the minister in all his activities by providing him with a clearer understanding of how to approach people for religion. It is significant that the most direct application of this approach—the field of evangelism—is showing in its literature a growing reliance upon the principles of counseling in winning people for the gospel.

Most of us have had a professor whose notes were yellow with age. He may have been a good teacher at one time, but his efficiency had lapsed with his notes. The notes may have been adequate at one time, but not having been revised, they had become dull as well as out of date. By neglecting to keep up in his field the professor had missed more than the new developments, for in his failure to grow he had lost his challenge. The result is that his use of his notes no longer carried the punch that it did when he first delivered them, even though the content was unchanged. No one deteriorates so fast or gets into a rut deeper than one who fails to keep abreast of his field.

The profession which to the layman seems to be most centered in practical experience is that of the medical doctor. After sitting in his waiting room by the hour, we can scarcely see how he can call his soul his own, let alone have time for scholarship. Yet some of the best of these physicians have regular study hours. One of the better clinics in my state has a weekly study night for its entire staff. They realize that medicine is not standing still and that the physician who ceases to read the current journals will soon find himself behind the times. The profession of the ministry is also in continuous change. This is especially true in the rapidly developing field of pastoral counseling. Regardless of how much seminary and clinical training a pastor may have had in his preparation for his counseling ministry, if he does not keep up to date in the contemporary publications, he will not only cease to improve, but he will reach a point where he will begin to regress.

Countering Resistance

So far as buying books or subscribing to professional periodicals is concerned, the pastor has no peer. So far as reading what he buys is concerned, this is another matter. "When do you get time to read?" he asks his brethren. Nor is it just a matter of reading. One can read and even read in his own field and still not be a student. Study requires time for thinking and evaluating, and this the pastor will never have without considerable effort. It is only as he realizes its worth that he will have the determination necessary to make this effort.

"I know I don't study enough," is an easy admission to get from a pastor. It is like "I know I don't pray enough"—or "I know I don't spend enough time with my family." These confessions are so readily made that we may question whether they are really confessions. According to the definition of confession that we give our people, one must not only confess his shortcomings but also intend to do something about them. This, we say, is the evidence of sincerity. The pastor usually makes his confession as though he were hopelessly trapped. There just is too much to do! The implication is that other activities of the ministry are more important and that scholarship has to give way. There is no judgment upon the pastor for this, because his conclusion is quite naturally reached. There is, however, the encouragement that the situation is not as impossible as it may seem. Scholarship can be worked into his program and without serious curtailment to other vital areas.

The ministry has been influenced by the value system of our activist culture. Because studying has no deadline that has to be met—no immediate results that must be reached—it succumbs before the demands of the appointment book and relinquishes its time to the things that just have to be done. There is no escaping the fact that the pastor is faced with a dilemma with his busy schedule, and we will take up this problem in the last chapter. Yet the pastor's stewardship of time may depend as much upon his anxiety about his program as upon the program itself. There is no apprehension over our study that preoccupies our mind as there is over our engagements and projects that involve other people. Consequently there is not the drawing power in study that there is in these pursuits that cause tension.

Much of our activistic emphasis must plead guilty to the subconscious conviction that everything depends upon us. If the pastor would deviate from his schedule, he may fear the whole program would collapse. The amazing thing is that the program seems to have a way of going on when the pastor is removed from the scene. Congregations have exhibited unforeseen stamina and resourcefulness during periods of pastoral vacancy. While the pastor would deny that he feels he is indispensable, his anxious pace indicates he feels he is quite important. In his attempt to do a great deal quantitatively, his quality begins to slip.

When the pastor's sights go beyond quantity to quality, he will see that study has its own definite place in the ministerial schedule. Particularly in the counseling area is quality a basic requirement. The pastor will improve the quality of his counseling when he improves the quality of his mental efficiency through a program of study. In addition, he will often find that things run more smoothly if he retires on occasion from the scene of action. The break has a way of refreshing him so that he is equipped for higher productivity when he takes part again. I have noticed that when I do a considerable amount of counseling without taking time to evaluate my work and check myself with somebody else's ideas, I tend to feel more and more authoritative and do more and more of the talking and make more and more blunders. When the quality of counseling increases, the quantity also increases. This brings its own unique crisis, which we shall take up in the last chapter.

A Systematic Program

Most of us become periodically concerned that we have been neglecting our scholarship. We may even become determined to do something drastic to change the situation. Like all good resolutions, this determination may become buried unless the pastor has a program for carrying it out. The important thing is not that he launch avidly into a book on pastoral counseling, but rather that he draw up a systematic schedule for reading that is realistically in line with his schedule of activities. Otherwise the spurt destroys itself through its intemperance. Reading periodicals is easier to handle than books because it provides an attractive diversion to sandwich in between activities or finish out the relaxation of the lunch hour. But reading a book is a long-term process. Since we cannot see the end in sight, we have a resistance to begin—at least with any thoroughness. Consequently discipline must replace whim as the means of execution. The pastor should select the books he wishes to study. The new books are regularly advertised and often reviewed in any national religious magazine, and the older classics find their way into the advertisements from time to time within these same periodicals. If the financial burden is too heavy, and his congregation does not provide for an expense account, his seminary library will help him out by mail.

The key to the success of his study plan is consistency rather than volume. Therefore, his next step is to determine the amount of reading he can manage on a daily, weekly, or monthly basis. This should include also the necessary aftereffects of his reading—time for reflection and absorption. Underestimating his quota insures better success than overestimating, since it avoids the danger of frustration. Whatever he may select— twenty-five pages a day, a book a week or every two weeks— should be allotted to a time of the day relatively free from other demands. This may mean early rising. Following a schedule, even though it is a modest one, gives the pastor a sense of security—things are under control. He is "on schedule."

Scholarship as part of the pastor's personal development for his counseling program includes also the study of his own counseling relationships. This means that he needs to write up the more significant of his interviews. Here also we run into the problem of time. The traditional suggestion that the pastor write up at least one counseling relationship verbatim seems to me to be too limited and time-consuming. I have found a typewritten summary of the interview on file cards to be more practical. In this summary I include the more significant data given by the counselee and whatever responses of my own that were particularly revealing so far as the counseling process is concerned. This would also include blunders. If through press I neglect to record an interview, I attempt to digest two or perhaps three interviews belonging to the same case at one sitting. Of course, it is much better to do the recording while the memory is still fresh, if this is possible. The file cards for each counselee whose interviews I am summarizing are clipped together and filed alphabetically. In his more difficult cases the pastor can study his notes and mentally structure his approach before the next interview. I find these notes excellent material for the pastor's own self-examination. Even the writing up of them fixes the insights of the hour in the pastor's mind. It should be remembered that these cards need to be placed where no straying eyes can ever peruse them.

The increasing opportunities for clinical training in pastoral care make it possible for the pastor to improve himself under skilled supervision. These courses are usually six weeks in length, five days a week, and conducted in an institution such as a hospital. Although counseling in an institutional setting may appear to be specialized, the principles of counseling are relatively uniform in their various applications. These courses are usually held during the summer, when he can absent himself during the week with the least amount of harm to the church program. The pastor can locate his nearest opportunity for clinical training by writing to the Institute of Pastoral Care or the Council for Clinical Training, under which most of these programs are co-ordinated.[1]

Finding the Balance

Of course, studying can be overdone as well as underdone. While they are in the minority, there are pastors who have to exert rigorous discipline to break away from books to inject themselves into the life of their congregation. Some of the church's finest counselors have been men who have had to force themselves to leave the peace and enjoyment of their scholarship to call in the homes of their people. Not all avid students are so moved by this constraint. As a result they lose out on the social end of their ministry and prevent the very opportunities for service for which their scholarship is to prepare them. What is needed is a balance. The minister's schedule is like the body of Christ, the church, of which it is a function. Each organ must work together with the other members, or the welfare of the body is sacrificed to the isolated development of one of its parts.

How can the pastor achieve this balance? The best way to

---

[1] Institute of Pastoral Care, Inc., Massachusetts General Hospital, Boston 14, Mass.; Council for Clinical Training, Inc., 2 East 103rd St., New York 29, N. Y.

get an accurate answer to this question is to put it in the negative: In what phase is he under par? We usually are only too well aware of our shortcomings because of our guilt over them. They have a way of developing out of previous patterns of emotional conflict. Since our conscience has a history of sensitivity to these shortcomings, it is quick to register when they occur. All we have to do is face the verdict without trying to rationalize its judgment. It is so easy for the pastor who dislikes calling to minimize the importance of calling, or the pastor who is too restless to study to delegate scholarship to the ivory tower, or the pastor who is afraid of counseling to say that things have a way of working themselves out if they are left alone.

Unless the conscience is distorted—under "the law of sin and death" rather than "the law of the Spirit of life in Christ Jesus" —it is a channel through which the Spirit of God operates his program of guidance. Instead of reacting to this voice of the Spirit as though it were a reproof, we may think of it as a suggestion. Rather than feeling defeated by the promptings of conscience, we can be inspired with hope. This means that when the pastor feels convicted of neglect in certain phases of his ministry, he should challenge this neglect, no matter what the consequences. Only by such a direct attack against the deficiency can he overcome the natural inertia that collects around any situation over which one feels guilty. His is the determination of one who has God as his Colaborer rather than his Judge.

We can see the value of the pastor's spiritual development as it relates to his growth in scholarship and in all areas of his ministry. Even as Christ is the Head of his church, so his Spirit is the moving force behind the minister. The minister's task is to keep his spirit sensitive to the Spirit so that he will receive the directions. The Spirit will evaluate and inform when we are determined to listen and willing to change.

Naturally there are times of exception when the pastor has an overload in services, such as in Holy Week, or in funerals, or in sick calls, or in critical meetings, and he has to sacrifice one phase of his work to handle the increase in the other. There is no harm in this temporary imbalance so long as it is temporary. The danger involved in making any exception to the rule is that the exception may become the rule. It takes on a momentum of its own which creates a resistance in the mechanics of personality to any change in pace when the crisis is passed. This development of inertia easily converts the emergency imbalance into a habit. This need not happen if the pastor understands the pattern and is determined to return to normal when the emergency has subsided.

CHAPTER ELEVEN

Managing His Own Household

ALTHOUGH THE PASTOR MAY REALIZE THAT GIVING ADVICE IS not the essential meaning of counseling, he nevertheless feels that he must be something of an example in those trouble zones for which his people seek his help. This is especially the case in the matter of family problems. Nor is this merely a figment of his mind. In his own Scriptures the qualifications for the bishop or overseer of God's church state that "he must manage his own household well, keeping his children submissive and respectful in every way; for if a man does not know how to manage his own household, how can he care for God's church?" (I Tim. 3:4-5, R.S.V.).

The marriage counselor whose wife divorced him may have contributed to the wit and humor of the day, but he hardly will attract people to his office for counsel. This in spite of the fact that he may follow the principles of counseling with accuracy and skill. We often quip at the unmarried pastor who must give marital counsel, but he is much better off so far as drawing appeal is concerned than the pastor who is obviously mismarried. The same is true for the pastor who has no children, as compared with the pastor whose children are severe cases of emotional disturbance.

Unnatural Pressure

The pastor realizes all this only too well. His marriage *must* be happy and his children *must* be exemplary if he is to give family and youth counsel. Any evidence to the contrary is a threat to his own standing, and he may react accordingly. Instead of being objective, he is defensive. Anxiously he seeks to make things look the way they should. He may resort to coercion to insure conformity. The demands of respect must be maintained at all costs. Without realizing it he may violate his own counseling procedure when he deals with his own family. Because he is driven by destructive emotions, he may break all the principles of psychology in the way he handles family crises. The result is that these problems grow worse instead of better. It is often when the situation becomes critical that the pastor first realizes his error.

We can easily see what others are doing wrong in their family situations because we are disinterested emotionally. But in our own family problems we can be amazingly blind to the causes. Our emotional involvement distorts our ability to discern our own role in these conflicts. The pastor may become too concerned about what other people—particularly his own congregation—may think or say to view the problem with the objectivity that is needed if he is to solve it. If his first procedure in counseling is to provide an acceptive atmosphere for the counselee, it must be because people prosper in this kind of relationship. Often he must try to counter the counselee's feeling of being unaccepted caused by the critical approach of the members of the counselee's own family. He knows that giving people the feeling that they are not accepted causes them to deteriorate emotionally. Yet he may do this very thing to the members of his own family.

In spite of his knowledge and experience as a religious person the pastor is not immune to the common problems of family life. Russell Dicks makes the bold statement that the number of pastors who are happily married would seem to vary little from the average, which he estimates at about ten per cent. Even if this estimate is low, it is still appalling. Dicks goes on to say that the pastor who is not happily married will not be effective in his counseling in this field.[1] When the pastor finds himself in the throes of marital and parental frustrations, he is also frustrated vocationally. The realization that he of all people should not be having these problems intensifies his suffering. More than even the opinions of others, the pastor is concerned about his own opinion of himself. When a man loses respect for himself, he is of all men most defeated. When a pastor loses respect for himself, his sense of failure is aggravated by the high standards of faith and life that the ministry implies.

Unnatural Results

The trouble starts with the pressure that the pastor feels from within and without to have the ideal marriage and family. There is a danger that he will try to use his family to satisfy this need. Appearance becomes the chief concern, while motives take a secondary role. The pastor's wife may experience this same pressure and be equally guilty in yielding her efforts to living a role rather than being a person. Their children's welfare then becomes undifferentiated from the satisfaction of the family pride. Although it may not openly be stated, this living-up-to-expectations philosophy of life is unmistakably the family code, and unconsciously they teach their children a subtle pharisaism. Either the children will go along with this superficial value scale, or they will become disgusted with it and may even rebel. In spite of the more scandalous behavior that may result, this course of resistance may be closer to the kingdom of God than that of conformity. The prodigal son came to himself, while the elder brother persisted in his moral blindness to the end. Actually such a child is rebelling against a role that is not real, a religion that is not Christianity, and a god that is not God.

[1] *Pastoral Work and Personal Counseling* (New York: The Macmillan Co., 1944), p. 82.

It is his determined effort to be honest regardless of whom he may hurt in doing it.

And so we have Bob, who represents the kind of "preacher's child" who has plenty of company. As a growing boy he felt that other children had plenty of money and plenty of freedom, and that he had precious little of either. Because he was prevented from participating in certain of the activities of those his own age, he felt different and out of things. He began to look upon his father's role of preacher with resentment. It seemed to him that he was walled in—caught in something he could not get out of—and he developed a touch of cynicism as he looked increasingly on the darker side of things. Bob wanted most of all to be free, to do what he wanted, to be himself. He felt exploited. "My folks want me to do the things that would bring honor to them, but they don't think about my satisfaction," he said. "They seem to want to make my decisions for me."

When he got away from home, Bob skipped church often. "It doesn't seem to make any difference whether I do or not. I still respect religion. I believe it is vital. But I don't seem to want it for myself." He has an emotional prejudice against what intellectually he believes in.

"I'm more interested in material things, it seems. And in having some fun. For some reason I feel I'm entitled to these things. I guess what religion I had was on the surface." Bob unconsciously sought out the type of friends and did the type of things that would dissociate him from the role he hated, because he believed it was cheating him out of the values he thought he desired. At the same time he felt the weight of guilt that he was disappointing his father and therefore God.

Here is a young man who is all mixed up inside. He is in need of pastoral counseling because of the mistakes of his pastor father and mother. Because of his emotional resistance to everything connected with the church, his receptivity to the counseling he needs is considerably blocked. Being a parent is one of the most difficult tasks asked of anyone, and who is the pastor who would say that Bob could not happen in his family? Yet in developing a counseling program in his church the pastor has to reckon with the warning that those who cannot handle their own problems can scarcely counsel with others. Simply having these family problems does not disqualify him. In fact, it is through these that he gains the wisdom of experience that makes him a better counselor. The issue that influences his counseling is whether he overcomes these problems or whether they overcome him. Some pastors probably feel bad about mistakes that have already been made. In their regrets they would give anything to be able to go back and correct them. Facing up to one's failures is part of the experience of life. When the pastor is able to do it and continue his work in the spirit of faith, he is still a valuable man for counsel, and people will know it.

The Need for Acceptance

The pastor's concern for his own reputation easily becomes confused with his pride. In his fear that his family will embarrass him, he may become overcautious in what he tolerates. This same dread causes him to be overcritical of his family's behavior. If this tendency were balanced by a positive fellowship between father and family, its effect would be minimized. But the pastor's busy schedule often prevents him from spending this necessary time with his children. The result is a family where there is too much father so far as restraint is concerned and too little father in the matter of fellowship.

According to the pastor's gospel the heavenly Father accepts his children as they are for Christ's sake. Through this approach he is able to give them the power to overcome their sin. When a person is criticized in a way that makes him feel unaccepted, he is hindered by guilt from taking any positive action. For this reason the forgiveness of sins is the prerequisite to living a Christian life. So the parent who criticizes his child until the child feels worthless makes him resentful toward the parent and leaves him feeling defeated. The stimulation of these destructive emotions moves the child to behavior that is even more unacceptable, and the parent reacts with increased hostility. So the vicious cycle in the deterioration of parent-child relationships.

To some extent the adage that he who governs best governs least applies also to parents. We need to have limits, and these should be held to. But too often the general consensus is that the pastor's family belongs to a higher morality. Our limits can be too restricted. Our ultimatums can be as childish as our children's. Discipline is not supported, but undermined, by overcorrection. The idea that more should be expected from the pastor's children than from the laymen's children leads to a tension that destroys the essence of Christian living. This superstandard extends even to grades in school and choice of vocation. "Let her alone," applies almost as much to the pastor's child as it did to Mary of Bethany. When he protects his children from this unnatural pressure by approaching their behavior apart from this pressure, he is giving them a chance to develop naturally, both emotionally and religiously. The pastor needs to accept his children as they are and enjoy them. Sanctification is a gradual process. God is working within them to will and do of his good pleasure, but unlike people, he does not expect them to change after one reprimand or even a lecture. We may hinder more than assist God in the nurture of our children when we discourage their confidence or provoke their resentment. We co-operate with him when we relax our tension over what other people are noticing so that we can appreciate our children for what they are; when we give them the love and affection that encourages them to respond to the voice of God; and when we teach them his Word in a way that encourages their freedom rather than stifles it.

Making Religion Appealing

Because of the close overlapping of the church and the home the pastor's family may develop a take-it-for-granted attitude toward religion. Religion tends to become inseparable from religious custom, so that doubts may not be recognized, or habit distinguished from experience. Because of this the challenge to make religion vital to the center of living is even greater in the parsonage than in the homes of the laity. Whatever has a negative effect upon the children in the religious schedule will make this challenge all the more difficult. The pastor and his wife cannot rely upon indoctrination or conformity alone to transfer religion from that which surrounds their family to something which each has as his own. This is the outcome of their efforts to make the religious activities of the family enjoyable to all.

This means that the spiritual life should not be pushed on the children as compensation for their deprivations. Sacrifices that are forced on us in the name of service to God may create a reaction within that breaks out destructively when the force is removed. They may also cause us to covet that which is denied. Nor is the spiritual life given a fair chance when it is presented as a substitute for the advantages and privileges of others. Whatever deprivations are necessary should be played down rather than magnified before the children, and the spiritual life should be kept free from any entangling alliances that would distort its appearance.

The gospel of grace was given not to create guilt but to put an end to it. The ideal is that law shall be swallowed up in love. Children who are the objects of continuous criticism feel guilty in simply being themselves. For them religion becomes a legal code rather than a gospel of acceptance. If our correction is patterned after the way the Holy Spirit corrects those who have experienced this acceptance, the purpose is not to make our children feel bad but to prevent them from hurting themselves, not to create in them a picture of failure but to help them find a better way.

The emphasis is on a positive future rather than on a negative past. This difference between a critical and evangelical approach to our children's conduct makes all the difference between a guilt that leads to forgiveness and progress and a guilt that leads to self-rejection and defeat.

Time for Marriage

Mark Twain said that no one knows what perfect love is until he has been married twenty-five years. The point is that marriages have to be built, and it takes time to build them. Yet being married twenty-five years is no automatic way to achieve this marital goal. Marriages meet their snags, and the pastor's marriage is no exception. It can endure these snags better than most others because of the extreme busyness of both parties. In many instances congregations get an assistant to the pastor free of charge in the pastor's wife. If there were more time and energy to face these areas of disharmony, they probably would create more disturbance. Yet it is these times when the distractions are removed that husband and wife are confronted with their problems, and this is step number one in solving them.

When the wife of a leading figure in the entertainment world divorced him for extreme cruelty, he did not contest. His wife, he said, was the family type, while he was married to his work. Because she resented this bigamy, he felt she had failed him as an understanding wife. The pastor's wife is much more understanding. She also finds herself married to man who is married to his work. The entertainer's attitude toward his marriage is the sort of thing a pastoral counselor would warn against in preparing such a couple for marriage, and yet he himself may be guilty of the same thing in the service of his church. He may even realize it, but raise his arms in despair. "What are you going to do?" he asks. "Which comes first—your family or your ministry?" And he has a point. Yet this much is sure—he is

131

not likely to develop his marriage to any great heights without devoting some time to it. And if he does develop his marriage, he will be a better counselor, when he tries to help others do this very thing.

His work is a divine calling. So also is his marriage. The marital vows are as sacred as are the ordinational vows. His wife deserves to be married to a husband, not to a congregation. If he really cannot develop the marital ties as God intended when he instituted the partnership—if his ministry is so all-consuming in time and energy that either his marriage or his work will suffer if he lives up to the vows of either—then there is only one conclusion: Roman Catholicism is right in insisting upon a celibacy of the clergy.

It may well be the pastor's tension rather than his work as such that makes marriage and the ministry a case of robbing Peter to pay Paul. His continual concern over tasks that are never completed, over responsibilities regarding others for time and eternity, makes it necessary for him to get away in mind and body from his work. It will help both his work and his marriage for him to take his wife out for a good time. His wife also will be in a better frame of mind for her roles as pastor's wife and mother after an experience of relaxation and enjoyment in the company of her husband. This in turn will help the children. It has been said of more than one pastor that he spent so much time in helping others' children that he neglected his own—and ultimately lost them. The pastor's responsibilities as a husband and father can be harmonized with his responsibilities as a minister—in fact, they must be harmonized if he is to do a good job in his ministry. The vital link between his own family experiences and his counseling program makes the latter dependent upon the former for its power.

As in his personal development through scholarship, so in his management of his own household, the pastor arrives at the common problem of finding a place for these things in his schedule. This is not an easy assignment, but through careful planning and organization it can be done. It will be our task to explore the mechanics of such an organizational program in the following chapter. When the pastor has achieved this balance in his activities, his counseling program will benefit. Beside the needed wisdom which scholarship and family living supply, they give also the confidence which goes along with wisdom. And confidence is most important for a counselor.

CHAPTER TWELVE

Solving the Dilemma of Busyness

We believe that this true church must be governed by the spiritual policy which our Lord has taught us in his Word—namely, that there be Ministers or Pastors to preach the Word of God, and to administer the Sacraments; also elders and deacons, who, together with the pastors, form the council of the Church; that by these means the true religion may be preserved, and the true doctrine every where propagated, likewise transgressors punished and restrained by spiritual means; also that the poor and distressed may be relieved and comforted, according to their necessities. By these means every thing will be carried on in the Church with good order and decency.

ALTHOUGH THIS ARTICLE (30) OF THE BELGIC CONFESSION IS nearly four hundred years old and expressed the Calvinist conception of church government, it is the familiar pattern recognized in most congregations today. Like an outline to which sub and sub-sub parts have later been added, it has become tremendously complicated in its modern setting. The office of the contemporary pastorate has become as impossible of fulfillment by one man as has the presidency of the United States.

An Eclectic Problem

The pastor is by no means a specialist. He must preach a new sermon once or twice each week to the same people; teach the Bible class on Sunday morning and the membership instruction classes during the week; work and plan with the young people's society; create and promote a progressive church program and persuade his vestry to accept it; call upon the sick and shut-ins and the dying; visit the prospective members, the delinquent members, the "peeved" members, and the good members; write up the parish paper; attend the socials and devotionals of the couple's club, the men's society, and sometimes even the women's societies; attend local conferences and co-operate in community enterprises; and perform the duties of a husband and father. In addition there are the funerals, the weddings (including the rehearsals), the continuous telephone conversations, and the letters to young people away from home. He carries the concern for the church finance program, the shortage of men in the choir, the need for teachers in the Sunday school, and maybe even a church building program. There are the evangelism-committee meetings, the Sunday-school board, the organizational planning committees, the denominational district committee, and state and national conventions. In the meantime he is supposed to be a student and a counselor.

When he goes to bed at night, the pastor's mind may be spinning with things that should be done. He lives continually under the pressure of a work that is never in check. Even if he keeps up with the daily needs, there are the many creative ideas that he is eager to try. Since he cannot possibly do it all, he must choose things that he feels are the more important. This brings up his scale of values. He will naturally tend toward those activities of the ministry that he feels are his forte. It is only logical that he should develop his talents. Yet whatever his speciality may be, his personal work with individuals is indispensable. He is a pastor in terms of the care of souls even before his role as an executive secretary of an institution.

Our talents are not always discovered without effort. There have been ministers who have felt a resistance toward pastoral work, but because of their realization of its necessity have worked hard at it and discovered they had a talent for it. One of the greatest of these was John Watson, also known as Ian

Maclaren. His Yale Lectures, published under the title *The Cure of Souls,* contained among other things a procedure for personal counseling out of his own rich experience in pastoral work. He was a gifted writer and preacher. Pastoral work, however, was very difficult for him. Through his tireless efforts he disciplined himself to become skillful at it. At the close of his days he said that if he had his ministry to do over again, he would give his people more consolation.

Horace Bushnell also found pastoral duties anything but easy. He also had talents in other areas. Yet when he faithfully performed his pastoral obligations, such as setting aside an evening each week for personal counseling, he became outstanding in this pursuit. His efficiency was abetted by the deepening of his own spiritual experience. He, like others who have worked at it diligently, discovered that there is no activity that is so rewarding to the minister. In the words of another great pastor, Charles Jefferson, there is no satisfaction that can compare with "the satisfaction of knowing that by an act of yours, one human life has been changed forever." [1]

The Psychology of Busyness

There may be more to busyness than simply having too much to do. It is one of the most acceptable escape mechanisms of our day. Our busyness may be a palliative to our conscience for failing to get at the things that we know we should do but toward which we have a resistance. There is a natural reluctance to do anything that is difficult. If the pastor has a tendency to look for escapes, he has one ready made for him in his impossible program. For example, if there is a marital situation that needs attention, he may convince himself with many infallible proofs that he will have to put this off until he gets some of the more pressing demands of his ministry under control. If pastoral

[1] Charles Kemp, *Physicians of the Soul* (New York: The Macmillan Co., 1947), p. 119. See also pp. 49-60.

work is difficult for him, he may point to his evenings filled with meetings as evidence that he cannot do it justice.

If we are using our busyness to justify our negligence, we may feel a touch of anxiety if our schedule should slow down. Since our busy schedule was the defense that was keeping our conscience from convicting us, a slack in the schedule would expose us to this fate. The mere prospect of this may throw us into a mild panic. The pangs of condemnation are more than many of us can take. When we are threatened with a slack, we may quickly look about for more assignments. This is why some people continually take on more than they can adequately handle. They create their own predicament by loading themselves down with responsibilities to prevent the anxiety that always comes with a vacancy. It is the only way they can avoid their fearsome obligations and still live with themselves.

Although some of us have succumbed more to the escape of busyness than others, few of us have not used it at one time or another. It is almost a part of the character of our culture. As we encourage our counselees to face their real motives, so we pastors will profit from a little self-analysis whenever we use busyness as a reason for negligence. If after an honest evaluation we believe there may be a tendency, no matter how slight, to use our busyness as a convenient escape, we are obligated to follow the course we would desire of our counselees and renounce the escape in favor of coming to grips with whatever we are reluctant to confront. It is only as we defy our weaknesses that we ever become their master. "Get behind me, Satan," is not only the weapon of defense which exposes the enemy, but also the weapon of attack that causes him to leave us for a season.

Following a Schedule

There is nothing about the busyness dilemma that determination and intelligent planning cannot solve. The key to efficiency is organization. The prerequisite of organization is a value system that reduces the less essential to make room for the more essential. Drawing up a time schedule is like drawing up a financial budget. A person will find plenty to do with his time without following a schedule, even as he will find plenty to do with his money without drawing up a budget. In either case the money and the time get spent. Yet the danger that essentials will be neglected is greater in not having a budget than in having one. The squeaky wheel may get the most grease even though it is a rather unimportant wheel, when the allotment of grease has not been apportioned in advance.

Since personal work is one of the *first essentials,* its place should be safeguarded by allocating the times for it in the weekly schedule. So far as the daytime is concerned, this would not be difficult. The conflicts arise in the evenings, when all the meetings occur. The evening is also the time when a certain amount of the calling and counseling should be done in order to reach those who are occupied during the day. Therefore, the pastor will have to designate a certain evening of the week for counseling and another for calling. He can explain to the congregation that these are set aside for the purpose and are unchanging except for emergencies. Although this may be a bit awkward at the beginning, in time it will become traditional, and the congregation will take it for granted.

Nor need the meetings suffer. Many pastors make excellent use of luncheon meetings. This is particularly applicable in urban areas, where lunch hours may coincide in a downtown business area. Where meetings are of necessity held in the evenings, it may not be necessary for the pastor to attend for the entire time. His most important time at the brotherhood meeting, for example, is after the meeting, during the refreshment informality. This is his opportunity for personal contacts. He may confer with the president of the organization beforehand by telephone concerning the business part of the meeting, and he may explain to any visiting speaker his reason for not being present during the program. Very few would consider this a discourtesy after an explanation. In mapping a schedule one is continually confronted with choosing the lesser of two evils or the greater of two goods.

What has been said concerning the brotherhood can also be said concerning other meetings, with the possible exception of the young people's society and the church council. Where the pastor has some item of business to present, he may arrange with the officers to make his report at a time that will offer him the maximum opportunity for using the evening for his other work. This of course depends upon a lay leadership that can function with some degree of independence.

Some pastors have found it helpful to check by telephone before making their calls to determine whether people will be at home. This is a great timesaver, especially when distance is a factor. There is the drawback, however, that the pastor may have more difficulty in making some of his visits if he gives the warning of a telephone call beforehand than if he confronts people at their front door. Also, as we have noted, such calls will lack the natural setting, at least at the beginning, that he might find if he called unannounced. It depends on how much the pastor relies upon timesaving devices to perform his obligations, whether he will use this method in his calling.

What has been said about the priority of personal work on certain evenings can also be applied to the primacy of study for the mornings. There is nothing like a disturbing telephone call to throw the pastor's mind into an emotional flare-up that makes further study impossible. What he needs is time free from these disturbances during the morning hours. And he should not have to rent a secret room, as some pastors have done, to get it. Even as the pastor should announce his hours for personal work, so also he should post his hours for study. It is beneficial for the congregation to know that the pastor does study. Although the announcement of his study time may not prevent all such interruptions (emergencies are excluded, of course), it will curtail many of them. Very few people will call at a time when they know he does not desire to be interrupted.

The organized life may bring about its own demise if it is not given occasional reprieves. Man is not a machine. His emotions can take just so much legislation before they rebel. There are few people who are so disciplined that they can direct their mental facilities with push-button efficiency. Most of us need to throw the schedule out on occasion. This is part of the purpose for the commandment for a Sabbath day. Man works better if one day out of the seven is free from the regular routine. The pastor needs to take this day off a week to obey the full meaning of the commandment. If he explains this to his congregation, they may think twice before calling him on the telephone on this day. Perhaps then he can lie in bed until he feels like getting up. This could be the day that he socializes with his family and friends, pursues his sport or hobby, or just lolls around the house to do whatever he feels like. The times when we "let down our hair" fulfill the need for freedom, even from a self-imposed schedule. They help to take the coercion out of our discipline and make us almost anxious to get back into schedule when the intermission is over.

Interruptions of his schedule come also from his ministerial activities. New churches have to be built; community and denominational demands interfere; out-of-town engagements crop up. These need do no permanent harm, for a schedule does not depend on rigidity for its success but rather on its resiliency to take these exceptions and return again to normalcy. We should not overlook the fact, however, that a sizable share of these extras are a commentary on our lack in lay responsibility. The pastor should be freed from duties that the laity can handle to do the things that distinguish his role from that of the laity. Although the void in lay responsibility is largely an inheritance from the past, the pastor can do much to change the situation. In most cases all the layman needs is the opportunity and the encouragement. If the layman is a businessman, homemaker, tradesman, salesman, farmer, teacher, there is no reason why his proficiencies cannot be coupled with the corresponding demands of the church. In some instances the pastor may have to train his laymen to do the things for which they feel unqualified.

The counseling ministry has an indirect role in the pastor's training of lay leadership. Through the counseling relationship the counselee learns to understand himself and his needs. He will be able to recognize the role of his emotional problems in the social irritations of church work. Whatever reduces the potentiality for friction among his lay workers reduces the flare-ups that create havoc with the pastor's schedule as he tries to repair the damage. The goal of the counseling process is the maturity of personality that enables an individual to assume responsibility. Besides helping these people to grow so that they can overcome their problems, the pastor is equipping them for service to the church program. This service may be assumed even during the counseling relationship and in a reciprocal way be the creative interest that assists the growth process. The rapport that the counseling process develops between counselor and counselee provides the basis for a smooth working relationship between pastor and lay worker.

If the pastor structures his role as a pastor to the congregation, he will make them conscious of the importance of his personal work. When they realize what he is trying to do with his time, they will be less likely to expect him to do what the lay leadership could and should do. They will understand when he explains why he cannot be present for this or that meeting in its entirety and will be more ready to assume the traditional duties, from mimeographing to custodial work, that subtract from a pastor's time in his role as a clergyman. Beside the help it would be to the pastor in his dilemma of busyness, this structuring will provide the layman with a much-needed understanding of the purpose of the ministry.

When They Come Too Fast

In attempting to solve the dilemma of busyness so that he may establish his counseling ministry, the pastor may find that his success with his counseling has created an imbalance that upsets his schedule. The seriousness of this threat is shown in the stories of counselors who have been literally swamped with counselees. Spurgeon had as many as thirty counseling sessions in one day. Phillips Brooks had a line of callers that began early in the morning. Our Lord himself was so besieged by those who wanted his help that he often had to plan his travels to keep ahead of this press that threatened to absorb his ministry. Among those who besiege the successful counselor may be some who are taking advantage of him—people who like the attention that comes from having one's problem the center of attention, people who bring the pastor matters of little moment which they could and should handle by themselves, people who choose to take their problem to the pastor as a substitute for the change they know they must make in their lives. Dr. Ellwood Worcester, whose deluge of counselees even upset his eating schedule, described his aim as "not to hurry them and not to allow them to waste my time." [2]

Usually it is not the members of his church alone who swamp the pastor, but people outside his flock who hear of his ability through his members and others. Although the pastor's first responsibility is to the congregation that has called him, he is obligated also to any "neighbor" in need. When he receives more requests for counseling than his schedule will allow, the pastor may find himself making his appointments a week or more in advance. This was my experience, and I believe is was a mistake. When people ask for counsel, they usually want to see the pastor right away. Their problem may involve some external crisis in which delay may be dangerous. Even if this is not the case, the psychological moment for counseling is when the individual asks for it. If he must wait a week before he can see the pastor, this moment may pass. With a typical change in mood he may have little desire to talk when the time comes, and if

[2] *Ibid.*, p. 116.

he returns at all, his indifference toward the interview hinders, if not entirely blocks the catharsis.

The better procedure is to work in this surplus between appointments. Though it may not be possible to get to the bottom of things in these few minutes, there is little time wasted in getting to the point, and the counselee at least expresses that part of his problem that most consciously agitates him. Even this brief catharsis gives him some relief. The pastor, on the other hand, has an idea of the gravity of the problem and can act accordingly. Of perhaps greatest importance, the counseling relationship has begun and will have a momentum of its own. The longer appointment can then be scheduled for a more convenient time. The wait in the meantime may also have a healing effect, particularly since there has been some catharsis. People often become greatly disturbed over incidents of the moment, but in a few days the emotions subside and the problem becomes of less importance.

During his counseling increase the pastor may also have to schedule half-hour appointments instead of the desirable hour. This is not good, but again it is the lesser of two evils, for it is also not good to allow the counseling ministry to swallow up other duties, such as sermon preparation. These are temporary measures during the emergency. Even one week may show a fluctuation in the number of counselees. The crests tend to level off even as do the troughs.

The principles of counseling are an ally in maintaining counseling efficiency to a maximum. By keeping the responsibility with the counselee the pastor offers no encouragement to him to use counseling for other purposes than growth. Those who attempt to use counseling for getting attention or as an escape from responsibility are obviously in need of help. The principles of counseling confront them with a structure that will give them this help if they are willing to adapt to it. Usually the process itself leads them to respond to its challenge without their conscious decision. The result is that they will grow toward a maturity that will enable them to require less of the pastor's time, or they will cease to come because they realize his type of counseling cannot be used to abet their desire to avoid responsibility. Although such people irritate the pastor, his faithful adherence to his principles will do more to counteract their exploitative tendencies than any show of impatience or stern rebuke. Also, this quality in the pastor's counseling will become known, so that any such abuse of it is often discouraged from the start.

Behind much of the strain that comes upon a pastor when his counseling hits its peaks is the impression of his own importance that these demands make upon him. He begins to think of himself as one with a burden of responsibility, and he may become anxious over whether he is doing all that he can for these people. The antidote for this strain is the realization of his own dispensability, which comes from an awareness of God as the one who works both through him and beyond him. Such a realization does not minimize his efforts nor reduce his efficiency, as may superficially be deduced. Rather, the opposite is true: faith produces works. By relieving the pastor of a burden that is not his to bear and of the resultant weariness of mind and body, this awareness not only makes him more available for divine guidance, but also reduces the frictions of fatigue and worry that slow down his mental processes.

When *Not* to Counsel

THE MINISTER WHO COUNSELS IS MORE THAN LIKELY TO BE confronted with people from time to time whom he is unable to help. Some of these may need psychiatric care. He needs to be able to recognize these cases so that he may assist in securing this help. From my own experience I would list the following as indications of the need for clinical psychology or psychiatry:

1. There are counselees whose problems seem to be within the scope of pastoral counseling, but who fail to respond after what both counselee and pastor feel is sufficient trial. This would not necessarily include those who seem to have a need for their problem but rather those whose problems appear to be buried too deeply for pastoral counseling to recover, or who have been handicapped by their emotional difficulties for so long a time that counseling is inadequate to release them. They may have been able to make a limited adjustment to life, but to make any genuine progress they need help to overcome their emotional handicaps, and the pastor's counseling has been unable to do this.

2. It is unfortunate but nevertheless true that some people come to the pastor's attention when they have deteriorated rather definitely so far as their mental functions are concerned. In certain emotional areas they can no longer distinguish between imagination and reality. Often it seems that the world

is full of devious plots against them. Although there is usually a core of truth to the things they relate, it is often rather fantastically embellished by the twisted way in which they perceive. Many of us may see things distortedly under severe stress, but theirs is a chronic distortion that makes it questionable how long they will be able to recognize reality enough to function in society.

3. There is a difference between a passing mood of depression and an acute siege of despondency. The inner agitations of the latter resemble the sufferings of severe physical pain. The counselee may feel that he cannot stand the distress any longer. His anxiety may become so intense that it is dissociated from any object of fear—having become the object in itself. The fact that he cannot account for his anxiety adds to it. The depression may be so intolerable that he feels like doing anything to escape from it. Therefore, there may be danger of self-destruction.

Probably the majority of people who indicate suicide thoughts to the pastor would never carry out these thoughts. Some obviously use such indications as threats to worry others or to hold their concern when they show signs of impatience. Also, most people at certain times in their life entertain thoughts of suicide. This is an immature but otherwise harmless phase in the periods of adjustment. The old adage, however, that those who talk about committing suicide are not the ones who do it, is not always true. When there are indications of something more than immature threats, the pastor may be wise to enlist the help of a psychiatrist.

Psychiatric help is not always just around the corner. In fact, many pastors, particularly in rural and small-town areas, are not at all sure about how to locate a psychiatrist. Some also, and with good reason, are concerned about having a psychiatrist whose ideas are at least sympathetic with Christian principles. One way to locate a psychiatrist is to ask the local medical doctor. Another way is to contact the social agencies of the community. The best insurance in locating psychiatric help of

Christian caliber is in contacting the nearest church social agency—welfare society, children's home, etc.; also the division of social welfare in the state and local councils of churches.

Not everyone who needs a psychiatrist is receptive to the idea. The old idea that going to a psychiatrist is an admission that one is "crazy" still exists in many sections of the country. The pastor can often be a help in persuading such people by referring to mental difficulties as emotional difficulties, which they really are—and by referring to a psychiatrist as a doctor. He can explain that the most important thing is that the counselee be helped, and that he himself may not be adequately trained to give this help. Even as we need a doctor when our bodies become ill, so we need a doctor when our emotions become ill. Because of these apprehensions over psychiatric help and the difficulties in obtaining it, he may on occasion also offer to arrange for the appointment or even to accompany the counselee to the doctor. While normally this would be considered too much support for the counselee, these obstacles may make it the lesser of two evils. In any event, it is well for the pastor as an interested professional to contact the psychiatrist who is treating his parishioner. Some psychiatrists actually prefer to work together with the pastor.

Psychiatry is no cure-all. It is an invaluable aid in the pastor's work, but it is no panacea to which he can send those whom he cannot help and for whom he is then no longer responsible. Psychiatrists also fail, or perhaps the patients fail the psychiatrist. Even those who are helped need to follow the ways of emotional health, or they will slip back into their old ways. In any case, people who visit a psychiatrist or who are patients at mental hospitals still need their pastor. The resources of the Christian religion are not exhausted even when the human sciences are inadequate. Nor need they be set aside while these sciences are at work.

Bibliography

Bonnell, John S. *Psychology for Pastor and People.* New York: Harper & Bros., 1948. The author has been actively engaged in pastoral counseling as a pastor of a large congregation for many years. He has been outstandingly successful, and his procedures should be known—but always in the context of Bonnell's distinct ability and long experience.

Dicks, Russell L. *Pastoral Work and Personal Counseling.* Revised edition. New York: The Macmillan Co., 1949. An easy-to-digest book on one authority's view of the nature of pastoral work. Dicks's emphasis is less on the science of procedure than on the nature of the task and the spirit of the pastor.

Doniger, Simon, ed. *Religion and Human Behavior.* New York: Association Press, 1954. A systematic grouping of articles appearing in *Pastoral Psychology,* by the editor, revealing the views of leading authorities both in psychiatry and in pastoral psychology concerning human nature and the relevance of religion and pastoral care to the functioning of the human psyche.

Dunbar, Flanders. *Mind and Body: Psychosomatic Medicine.* New York: Random House, 1947, A classic in the relationship of the ills of the soul to the ills of the body. An aid to the pastor to perceive the spiritual need behind the physical illness.

Hiltner, Seward. *Pastoral Counseling.* New York and Nashville: Abingdon Press, 1949. This book and the volume by Carroll A. Wise are the two best books on the method of pastoral counseling at the present time.

————.*The Counselor in Counseling.* New York and Nashville: Abingdon Press, 1952. An aid to self-analysis for the pastor. Hiltner shows by actual interviews how the attitudes of the counselor affect the outcome of the counseling process.

Hulme, William E. *Face Your Life with Confidence.* New York: Prentice-Hall, Inc., 1953. A book of counsels for youth in which the pastoral-counseling interview is used as a vehicle to help the reader to assume the role of counselee.

Johnson, Paul E. *Psychology of Pastoral Care.* New York and Nash-ville: Abingdon Press, 1953. A comprehensive and detailed study of the total pastoral task in the light of modern psychological in-sights and with a specific emphasis upon counseling—by one en-gaged in the teaching of pastoral counseling for many years.

Kantonen, T. A. *The Theology of Evangelism.* Philadelphia: Muh-lenberg Press, 1954. This little book is a help to the pastor in re-lating the classical theology of Christianity to his personal work, both in evangelism and in counseling.

Kew, Clifton E., and Clinton J. Kew. *You Can Be Healed.* New York: Prentice Hall, Inc., 1953. A minister and a psychologist team up to develop and present a program of counseling in groups. The setting for much of their work is within the frame-work of the local congregation.

Künkel, Fritz. *In Search of Maturity.* New York: Chas. Scribner's Sons, 1943. The author guides the reader to depths in both in-sight and experience as he relates God and the Christian gospel to the release of the destructive emotions that block human growth.

May, Rollo. *Man's Search for Himself.* New York: W. W. Norton & Co., Inc., 1953. A profound and disturbing book. The author pre-sents the meaning of Christian sanctification in the language and thought forms of modern psychotherapy. An analysis of the emptiness, loneliness, and worthlessness inherent in the anxious nature of our age.

Oates, Wayne E. *The Bible in Pastoral Care.* Philadelphia: West-minster Press, 1953. A guide in the general use of the Bible in personal work, together with a selection of specific Bible passages for specific needs.

Outler, Albert C. *Psychotherapy and the Christian Message.* New York: Harper & Bros., 1954. A commendable job in comparing the philosophies of leading psychoanalysts with Christian con-cepts, showing the similarities and divergences.

Roberts, David E. *Psychotherapy and a Christian View of Man.* New York: Chas. Scribner's Sons, 1950. This little book is similar in aim to the book by Dr. Outler. It is, however, more limited in scope, in its treatment of both psychotherapy and Christian doctrines.

Schuette, Walter E. *The Minister's Personal Guide.* New York: Harper & Bros., 1953. A wise old pastor's pastor gives practical counsel to the minister concerning his personal behavior—the "little things" in ethics and decorum that play a significant role in establishing a counseling ministry.

Wise, Carroll A. *Pastoral Counseling: Its Theory and Practice.* New York: Harper & Bros., 1951. This book is scientifically presented. Although it lacks the illustrative material of Hiltner's volume, it is surprisingly good reading.

Periodicals

Pastoral Psychology. Great Neck, N. Y. A monthly periodical devoted to the application of dynamic psychology and religion to the gamut of human experiences—with special reference to the pastoral role.

The Journal of Pastoral Care. Andover Hall, Cambridge, Mass. A quarterly journal sponsored by the Institute of Pastoral Care and the Council for Clinical Training to foster the relationship of psychology and theology in pastoral work, with specific emphasis upon interprofessional relationships and clinical pastoral training.

Index

INDEX